ROUTLEDGE LIBRARY EDITIONS: URBAN AND REGIONAL ECONOMICS

Volume 1

REGIONAL ECONOMIC PROBLEMS

REGIONAL ECONOMIC PROBLEMS

Comparative Experiences of Some Market Economies

A. J. BROWN AND E. M. BURROWS

Routledge
Taylor & Francis Group

LONDON AND NEW YORK

First published in 1977 by Allen & Unwin

This edition first published in 2018
by Routledge
2 Park Square, Milton Park, Abingdon, Oxon OX14 4RN

and by Routledge
711 Third Avenue, New York, NY 10017

Routledge is an imprint of the Taylor & Francis Group, an informa business

British Library Cataloguing in Publication Data
A catalogue record for this book is available from the British Library

ISBN: 978-1-138-09590-8 (Set)
ISBN: 978-1-315-10306-8 (Set) (ebk)
ISBN: 978-1-138-10214-9 (Volume 1) (hbk)
ISBN: 978-1-138-10247-7 (Volume 1) (pbk)
ISBN: 978-1-315-10330-3 (Volume 1) (ebk)

Publisher's Note
The publisher has gone to great lengths to ensure the quality of this reprint but points out that some imperfections in the original copies may be apparent.

Disclaimer
The publisher has made every effort to trace copyright holders and would welcome correspondence from those they have been unable to trace.

Regional Economic Problems

Comparative experiences of some market economies

BY

A. J. BROWN

AND

E. M. BURROWS

University of Leeds

London

GEORGE ALLEN & UNWIN

Boston   Sydney

First published in 1977
Second impression 1979

GEORGE ALLEN & UNWIN LTD
40 Museum Street, London WC1A 1LU

ISBN 0 04 339010 2 hardback
0 04 339011 0 paperback

Printed in Great Britain at the
University Press, Cambridge

PREFACE

The literature of regional economics has grown large in recent years, and in offering an addition to it (especially one with a fairly general title) we ought perhaps to state as clearly as possible both what the book attempts and what it does not attempt.

To start with the latter, it makes no attempt to give a general survey of, or introduction to, the techniques that have been evolved under the headings of regional analysis or regional science – in effect, the techniques of constructing formal models of economic activity in which space or distance play a principal part. Books on these techniques are already in good supply.

On the other hand, we hope we have provided something more than a descriptive survey of some economic problem areas and, briefly, of the policies that have been applied by governments to deal with them. Our approach is related to policy, but it starts with the fundamental question (often unasked, or raised only as an embarrassing afterthought): what are the grounds for having a regional policy at all? It is a question which cannot be answered without some general, theoretical notions of the ways in which regional problems can arise.

Having considered what constitutes a satisfactory answer to this question, we first make a very short general survey of the main kinds of problem region with regard to which a convincing case for policy arises – taking, as throughout the book, a region to be a major division of a country, not simply any small area that happens to attract attention by reason of its difficulties. We then consider in greater detail, and with the aid of some brief case studies set in the context of world economic change, four of the commoner types of problem region that are to be found in the more developed market economies – agricultural problem regions, coal-mining problem regions, old manufacturing (specifically, textile-manufacturing) regions, and regions that are held to present a problem of congestion. Finally, and very briefly in relation to the breadth of the subject, we examine the styles, methods and effectiveness of regional policies that have emerged in some of the principal more or less free-market economies, especially those from which our case studies of problem areas are drawn. We have not included the problem regions or regional policies of the advanced centrally planned economies; the circumstances both of economic change and of decision making in them are different from those in the countries where regional policy has been most explicitly a public issue, and to bring them properly into our picture would be a major task, which we have not thought it practicable to perform within our limited space.

For the reader who wants to go further, we hope that our highly selective bibliography at the end will be of some help, but in our presentation we have aimed at readability rather than either scholarly and detailed attribution throughout the text to the numerous sources to which we are indebted, or the provision of a statistical base from which further analysis might proceed.

The major debt we must acknowledge at the outset, however, is to the Nuffield Foundation, for its great generosity in offering, spontaneously, a Research Fellowship without which work on this book could not have proceeded at all with any hope of ever being finished. Our gratitude is due also to the University of Leeds for providing not only the physical surroundings in which the work was done, but the stimulus of colleagues and students to discuss it with. Finally, we record our thanks to Ruth Brown, who drew the maps.

CONTENTS

9

MAPS

CHAPTER 1

What are Regional Economic Problems?

Like all economic problems that are important in practice, regional economic problems are matters that worry people or governments in connection with the ordinary business of earning a living, or sometimes in political or social connections related to it. What makes them 'regional' is simply their being concerned predominantly with a major division of a country, or with the relations between the affairs of different major divisions of it. Most commonly they arise from economic grievances that are felt by the people, or by important sections of the people, in such major divisions; that is to say in particular regions. Less often they spring, not so much from the worries of people in particular regions, as from a more general concern of national opinion, or the central government, with the distribution of economic activity and population between regions. They are economic problems with a spatial basis of the particular kind that we normally call 'regional'.

WHAT ARE REGIONS?

What we mean by 'regional' perhaps needs a little further clarification. It has already been implied that a region (in the sense in which we shall use the term) is a major division of a country. This, in turn, has two implications. First, we are talking, not about separate sovereign states, but about areas that lie under the jurisdiction of a wider national government, which is expected to be concerned about their welfare, but is similarly responsible for that of other regions as well, and may have to balance conflicting regional interests against each other. Apart from this, there are the further economic implications of the fact that the regions of a country have in some ways closer relations with one

13

another than separate countries have. In particular, they usually enjoy a common monetary system and freedom of trade and of movements of capital and labour between themselves. This rules out some of the policy expedients – tariffs, exchange control, alteration of exchange rates – that play parts in the economic inter-relations of separate countries. It also means that some of the assumptions that have customarily been made in order to arrive at a first theoretical understanding of international economics are not plausible, even for a start, in regional economic analysis. The economic relations between regions are different from those between countries, and still more different from those postulated in classical international trade theory.

The other specification that has been implied is that the regions we are concerned with are *major* divisions of a country. This is really a matter of convenience. Countries differ enormously, of course, both in size and in the variety of localised economic communities that they contain, but in most of them there is some sort of awareness of a small number – usually from two to a dozen – of spatially distinguishable divisions, different in economic respects that bear upon national policy. Beyond them there lie an indefinite number of smaller divisions, sometimes with very clear differences of welfare and interest – separate towns and rural districts, working-class and middle-class suburbs, manufacturing and shopping districts and so forth – which we exclude from this discussion for a variety of reasons. It is, however, perfectly adequate to say that we exclude them because they are too numerous. We are not concerned here with the whole range of spatial economic problems that arise inside a country, down to the problems of urban and local economies that bear on town and country planning usually carried out by local authorities. We are concerned only with the top layer of spatial problems, which are *essentially* central government concerns to a substantial extent.

That, however, is clearly not all that there is to be said about what constitutes a 'region' for our purpose. The question is indeed, naturally very widely discussed, especially whenever reform of local government is in the air. At first sight, there seem to be two main principles on which economic regions might be delimited: a region might be conceived either as an area in which all the parts have as far as possible similar economic structures – and therefore similar predominant economic problems and interests – or it might be so delimited as to be, as far as possible, not highly dependent on transactions with other

14

regions. In an advanced economy, with a strong internal division of labour, self-sufficiency in a region probably implies that its separate sub-regional parts are complementary to each other, and therefore *different* in their structures, problems and interests. The two principles look, therefore, as if they are antithetic to one another.

In fact, it is not as simple as this. The areas that are most homogeneous within themselves and most different from one another are usually the very small ones, such as rural districts or particular kinds of residential neighbourhood, which are much less than regional in extent. In most countries (certainly in the more developed ones) any area big enough to qualify as a region will contain a rich variety of sub-regional areas with different economic structures. For almost any practical purpose for which economic regions are to be distinguished, it will be appropriate to put together the sub-regions that are complementary, and have most to do with each other, least with the rest of the country. But that does not exclude a wide community of economic problems and interests within a region composed in this way. Indeed, a region that forms an organic whole in the sense that its sub-regions are complementary with each other will have a common interest in the fortunes of the industries that sell to the outside world. The prosperity of these industries, depending largely on the state of demand for their products, and the degree of competition from other regions that produce them, affects the demand for all the other goods and services that the region produces. Some regions are dependent in this way on the external demand for a very limited range of products. One has only to think of the extent to which the west midlands depends on motor cars, the deep south of the United States on raw cotton and tobacco, or Nordrhein-Westfalen on coal and steel, though these are (and were) regions of considerable diversity, with urban and rural parts and wide ranges of industries.

Regions are, therefore, sometimes delimited in accordance with the interests and the economic character that come from their predominant export industries. It is an advantage if they can be so defined that big daily movements of people travelling to work – or, for that matter, any frequent but regular large movements, such as those for shopping and entertainment – do not take place across their boundaries. These movements are among the main activities that bind neighbouring areas together economically.

But what makes it inevitable that a particular area is treated as a region in practice is often, immediately, not an economic characteristic at all but social or political; for example, that all or most of the people in it share a consciousness of belonging to a single community. A consciousness of this kind is, of course, often produced by the economic circumstances that have been referred to – the dependence directly or indirectly on a particular industry or group of industries producing (again, directly or indirectly) for the outside world. (In the simplest cases it may spring from difference of predominant occupation and way of life – especially in regions that are mainly agricultural or mining or urban.) But it may spring from quite different factors: language or manner of speech, religion or sect, race or tribe, traditional memory of things done or suffered – in short, from all the influences that, with the addition of an aspiration to complete political dependence, make a national consciousness.

These factors can produce regional boundaries that have very little purely economic validity. Wales, for instance, consists not only of the coalmining valleys of the south, and the surrounding countryside that looks to Cardiff and Swansea – a very well-marked regional community – but also of central Wales, looking economically to the west midlands, and north Wales looking largely to Liverpool and Manchester, and only minimally connected, economically, with South Wales or, indeed, with each other. Yet, politically and administratively these economically distinct parts of Wales have to go together, because most of them are too small to qualify for separate regional status, and important parts of their populations would presumably find their sense of Welshness affronted by a proposal that they should be amalgamated with any English region. For many reasons of this kind, the regions for which we have separate economic data, and indeed, the regions that have coherent voices and senses of common interest, are not always those that conform best to the notion of major economically distinct communities, and for economic analysis we have to make do with the regions we have.

REGIONAL GRIEVANCES

With this qualification, what are typically 'regional' economic problems? First, as we have noted, they are the states of affairs about which predominant opinion in regions feels a sense of communal grievance; second, they are the matters touching

16

regional economic welfare about which the central government, or predominant or national opinion, feels some unease. Let us look at the grievances first. There is an understandable tendency for the people of a region to complain if average incomes in it are noticeably lower than in other regions of the country, or if they are increasing noticeably less fast (still more, if they are actually declining). Similarly, and for obvious reasons, regional communities complain if they suffer higher rates of unemployment than prevail elsewhere. There are complaints if there is what is thought to be an unduly high rate of net outward migration, still more if it is such as to cause an actual fall in population. There may be complaints, in the absence of important *net* emigration, if there is a large outward flow of the young and vigorous or the better-educated which is partly or wholly offset by an inflow of (say) retired people. There are apt to be widespread senses of grievance in a region whenever central government economic policy is thought to be such as to discriminate against it. The three circumstances first mentioned – relatively low incomes, relatively high unemployment and net outward migration – are, of course, often found together. They are aspects of a relative poverty of economic opportunity in a region.

The reasons why these circumstances should lead to some sense of regional grievance are mostly obvious enough. That the economic opportunities in one's region are inferior to those elsewhere may be hurtful insofar as one is unable to move to the richer pastures, or so attached to home that one is reluctant to do so, or so identified with one's community that one feels a sense of injustice on its behalf. Where there is heavy net outward migration people who stay at home may regret its effect in diminishing (or simply in changing) communities to which they are emotionally attached, or they may dislike its effect on the local markets, or other sources of revenue, on which they depend economically – or both.

But how far these grounds for grievance constitute grounds for *national* concern, justifying some attempt by policy to redress the grievances or to remove their cause, is another matter. To decide that, one must look at their implication for the country as a whole.

Inequality of incomes

Inequality of personal incomes between regions gives *prima facie* cause for concern, just as does *any* inequality of incomes, on the general ground that welfare would be greater if the same total income was more evenly distributed – a given loss by the better-off would hurt them less (simply because they *are* better off) than an equal gain would benefit the poorer. But in most economies income differences between individuals within any region are very large in comparison with differences between regional *average* levels. On any reasonable assumption about the rate at which the subjective value of an extra pound of personal income falls off as personal income rises, it can be shown that the potential benefits of equalising all incomes within any region would be many times greater than those of equalising *average* income levels between two regions – even if in one of those regions average income was initially twice as high as in the other one.

Usually, indeed, the differences in *average* incomes between, say, a poor working-class neighbourhood and a well-to-do middle-class neighbourhood in a city will be much bigger than the differences of average income between any two regions of the country. Relatively, therefore, the latter differences may not seem to give much to worry about on grounds of equity. The fact remains, however, that a government may have to take notice of inter-regional differences if the people of the less fortunate regions are sufficiently aware of them, even if it believes that awareness to be out of scale with the feelings about other inequalities in the community.

The other ground for national concern about inter-regional income differences arises from their significance as symptoms of a mislocation of productive resources. If labour earns less in a given occupation in one region than in another, there is a presumption that output could be raised if some workers moved to the higher paying region. In the same way, if the rate of profit on capital is higher in a given industry in one region than in another, it can be argued that total product would be increased if the distribution of plant could be shifted in favour of the higher profit region. If the region of higher profit is the region of lower wages and salaries, the presumption is that labour and capital are mislocated in relation to each other, and that shifts

18

either of labour in one direction or of capital in the other, or both together, would raise total output. If both labour and capital are earning less in a given industry in one region than another, the presumption is that the lower earning region is a poorer location for that industry – perhaps because of less favourable natural environment, or greater effective distance from markets or supplies or services. If this presumption is justified, it follows that there should be a gain in production if both the industry in question, or some of it, and some labour moved to the more favoured region.

There are, of course, some qualifications to these simple presumptions. Low wage earnings in a region may be due, not to a relative excess of labour, nor to poor location of industry, but to inferior levels of skill, or of education, or to general attitudes towards the work and organisation of the industry in question that make for lower productivity in it. Some of these, no doubt, are still causes for national concern, but they do not necessarily call for shifts of population or industry. Deficiencies of skill and education in a region call for a redistribution, or a supplementation, of educational and training facilities. Differences in attitudes to work are another matter; if some communities (like some individuals) value leisure or personal independence more highly in relation to income than others do, there is no obvious reason why governments, or anyone else, should be concerned about it, so long as the people in question do not expect to have the extra leisure (or independence) and parity of income as well. The trouble is that they sometimes do.

There are qualifications to be made also when regions differ in average earnings because of differences in the balance of occupations within them. Different occupations command different earnings for a variety of reasons. Some carry high pay because they require personal qualities that are naturally scarce, some because of their special unpleasantness or danger, some because social and institutional factors restrict entry into them, and some because demand is shifting towards them and recruitment responds with less than perfect freedom. The first two and in a rather lower degree the third of these grounds for inter-occupational difference are durable and pervasive. In most communities, moreover, they are broadly accepted, subject to whatever arrangements may be in force for redistributing income through taxation and the social services. The concentration of a high proportion of the high earning occupations or those demanding higher educational standards in a particular region (usually the metropolitan one) is often, however, less happily accepted. Objection to it may be well founded insofar as this kind of distribution causes antipathies between classes and senses of separateness between regions to reinforce each other, and produce a divided country. This in turn may restrict inter-regional mobility or, in extreme cases, lead in the direction of secession. It may also be well founded insofar as the cultural and other facilities of which the better-off or the better-educated are the strongest patrons become unduly concentrated in the metropolis, or wherever such people are mostly to be found. This contributes further to geographical separation of cultures; it also hinders the growth of the regions of lower income and educational standards by making them less attractive to. the managerial and professional classes. This, in turn, also tends to make the cultural divisions of the country self-reinforcing.

Against these disadvantages of regional separation of occupations and cultures one has to set the advantages of efficiency that come from geographical concentration in the professional and cultural fields. How far does it benefit the whole country, by giving efficiency in administration, if all the central government departments are in the same city – or at least the same region? How far does it help smooth working if the head offices of firms are there, too, including the head offices of the banks? Or the capital market (if there is one) and the main commodity markets? Or the main institutions of higher education and research establishments? How far does a heavy concentration of this kind make possible, for instance, concerts, plays and art exhibitions of a quality that could not be maintained if the population with relevant interests were more widely dispersed through the country? These are difficult questions. If they can be answered, the advantages of concentration of the high-earners and the highly-educated that they reveal have to be balanced against the strains of inter-regional inequality based on occupational difference.

Where differences in occupational rewards are simply due to shifts in the balance of demand, coupled with frictions of movement, they are perhaps less willingly accepted as being inevitable or fair. The concept of 'the rate for the job', uniform throughout the community, is a simple and appealing one. But, economically, it cannot be accepted without reservation. The place where the job is done may be as relevant to the wider assessment of its social usefulness as the rest of the job specification. This can obviously be so where the work in question is connected with the production of something that is essentially immovable – a house, a road, or a personal service to members of a resident population. These things, at a given time, may be needed more in one place than in another. But it is also true of the production of movable goods. Clearly it is true of them insofar as they are not perfectly movable – there are costs of moving them and the materials that go into them, and the total of such costs is lower if they are produced in some places than in others. Even if one can ignore these transport cost differences, however, it may still be true that the contribution of a particular labour unit to production is more valuable in one place than in another, because labour units of that particular kind (men with skill in a particular trade, say) are scarcer in the first place than in the second in relation to all the other necessities for the kind of production in question. Industrial labour and industrial workplaces may not be distributed geographically so as to match each other.

These conditions in which the social usefulness of a particular job is not the same in different parts of the country are, in fact, conditions of less than perfect distribution of resources. With an ideal distribution of labour and capital, a given kind of labour would have the same marginal social product wherever it exists; so would a given kind of industrial plant, or a given variety of social capital. Areas with special advantages for production and residence, with natural environments favourable to both, considered together, would be well supplied with both population and capital; areas with less advantageous endowments of resources would have less of both. People and capital would always be adjusted in supply both to natural resources (in the widest sense) and to each other. And, given that the markets for labour and capital were not noticeably more imperfect in one region than in another, 'the rate for the job', and the rate of return on a given kind of capital, would be the same everywhere.

Actual situations, in which this ideal is not achieved, imply some loss of social product in comparison with the ideal situation. They carry the implication that some rearrangement of labour and capital is possible that would take people and/or units of capital from places where their marginal products are lower to places where they are higher, thus raising the total social product. The existence of considerable inter-regional variations in 'the rate for the job' or in the rate of profit in particular industries is *prima facie* evidence for this kind of lapse from the 'ideal' geographical distribution of resources.

How serious a lapse is it? In the terms in which we have stated the problem, probably not very serious. Inter-regional differences of (say) 20 per cent, which are not uncommon, can be shown, on simple but not absurd assumptions, to imply very small losses. If, starting with such differences in its marginal product (which we will assume wages to represent reasonably well), labour were to move towards the regions of higher earnings, the presumption is that the consequent changes in the degree of scarcity of labour in relation to other factors of production would soon extinguish the differences. The number of movers, whose increases in marginal product would constitute the gain to society, would generally not have to be very great (in proportion to the total labour force) to bring this about, and the increases in question would, of course, tail off to zero in the process.

This is true so long as there is a tendency for production methods to be adjusted to take account of the relative local supplies of capital and labour, so that both are fully employed. If, on the contrary, there is a fixed ratio between capital and labour requirements, so that any departure of local supplies from this ratio results in either unemployed labour or unfilled vacancies, then the loss that these results entail is very much greater. To have labour earning relatively poorly because its marginal product is low is a great deal better than to have it not earning at all, and the same is true of other factors of production. Inter-regionally unequal earnings and full employment of resources is better (in the simple sense of implying a larger total social product) than an imposed equality of earnings that results in any substantial degree of unemployment.

Unemployment differences

It is obvious enough, too, why communities do not like having rates of unemployment that are higher than those elsewhere, more particularly when the general level of such rates in the country is such as to cause unease. Officially published unemployment rates are not always easy to interpret. They can, for instance, be high either because a lot of people are subjected to the risk of relatively short average periods of unemployment, or because a relatively small number of people (those displaced from a declining industry, for instance) face the prospect of long periods without a job or in some cases no visible prospect of re-employment at all. Their scope varies from country to country; in the United Kingdom they include only those who are insured against unemployment and have registered as unemployed, thus excluding a large number of (for instance) married women, not so insured, who have had jobs but have lost them. In the United States, they are based upon sample surveys among the whole population of working age, and thus come nearer to assessing the proportion of the potential workforce who are not at the time in a job, but are looking or hoping for one. Everywhere they exclude people (many housewives, in particular) who in different labour market conditions or a different climate of opinion might go out to work, but actually do not regard themselves as seeking to do so.

But whatever the ambiguities and imperfections of an unemployment rate as a measure of involuntary worklessness, it provides, in any given country, some kind of indicator of the variation in an important aspect of economic opportunity between one region and another. Higher unemployment than elsewhere is apt to mean, for many people, employed or unemployed, a higher expectation of voluntary worklessness during any future period – less security for those in work and less hope for those seeking it.

These lower levels of security and hope must be counted as very substantial parts of the social cost of a relatively high unemployment rate in a particular region, though they are, of course, hard to quantify. What is much easier to quantify is the potential output lost through the actual unemployment existing in any given period – what the unemployed people might have produced (in value-added terms) if they had been in work. Production losses from involuntary worklessness other than registered unemployment are harder to assess because we know less about its extent. Sources of information about people not registered as either having jobs or seeking them are usually imperfect; it is often not clear whether they are in fact productively occupied. Losses that arise because, for instance, chronic slackness of demand for labour in a region has meant that many housewives have never thought of seeking jobs (though they are in principle free to do so) are harder to judge still. All these losses of production may be real ones in a region where demand for labour is persistently less than supply of it, but it would be a mistake to regard them as exhausting the social costs of such demand deficiency; the pervading sense of insecurity and hopelessness it engenders, to which we have referred, has to be considered as well.

But what we are considering is not high unemployment and low demand for labour as such; it is inter-regional differences in them that present governments with specifically regional problems. Objectively, from the national viewpoint, is there more loss of production and more damage to morale from having a 1 per cent unemployment rate in one half of the country, and 5 per cent in the other half, than in having a 3 per cent rate everywhere? The answer is clearly 'Yes' in either of two cases – if there are costs connected with having unemployment rates *below* a certain level, as well as with having them above it, and if the cost and damage associated with a high unemployment rate rises more than in proportion to it.

Either or both of these cases may arise. In practice, there is some finite rate of unemployment that corresponds, in any region, to the 'best' balance for production between supply of manpower and demand for it. To get to lower rates of unemployment than this will create a manpower shortage so acute that the loss of potential production from unused or under-used equipment outweighs the gain from the accompanying diminution in the amount of unused labour. If one thinks in terms of labour alone, it is still true that it can be 'wasted' just as much indirectly, through the non-use of equipment it has produced, as directly, through lack of appropriate equipment for it to use. Shortage of demand for labour in high-unemployment regions means absence of jobs (i.e. workplaces equipped to produce what the market will take at an appropriate price); shortage of labour in low-unemployment regions can mean absence of direct labour to make full use of equipment that has been installed. The loss from the mismatch between labour and equipment is a double one.

As for the human impact of unemployment, if it gets worse with the duration of the workless period (as seems likely because of the limited size of financial and other reserves, and of human resilance), then it is likely to be worse to have a given amount of unemployment concentrated in one part of the country than to have the same amount spread evenly over it, where concentration in (say) one region is likely to mean longer spells out of work for those who suffer unemployment – the average duration and incidence of unemployment in a community tend to rise together. The more a given unemployment total is concentrated on part of the nation, too, the more likely it is that two or more people in the same household will be affected by it at the same time, or within a given period. Unemployment-induced poverty will be more unevenly spread. There seems to be some reason, therefore, for thinking that a given volume of unemployment is more damaging the more it is concentrated in particular communities.

The most frequently argued case for spreading a given volume of unemployment (if a certain level is inevitable) fairly evenly between regions has, however, been a different one, connected with inflation and the management of the economy to avoid or mitigate it. The contention is that inflation of the kind promoted by the raising of wages in the labour market, and the passing-on of this rise into the prices of products, is accelerated by lower rates of unemployment, slowed down by higher ones. The inflationary effect of a given decrease of unemployment in a low-unemployment region, however, is held in this view to be greater than the counter-inflationary effect of an equal increase of unemployment in a high-unemployment region.

Since rates of wage increase do not, in fact, diverge very much between regions in some countries, in spite of big unemployment differences, it is perhaps more realistic to suppose, for those countries, that the regions of relative labour shortage set the pace for wage increase, and that the others tend to follow them. If this is so, and if the pace of inflation in the absence of this imitative tendency would tend to be hotter where labour is shorter, it follows that, with a given national unemployment total, inflation tends to be faster the more unevenly the unemployment is spread.

But while inflation is undeniably a nuisance, creating public alarm and recurrent balance-of-payments crises in the circumstances with which the most advanced countries have been familiar in recent times, its real cost is elusive. One can say much more confidently that, if governments know, or find, that they have to regulate the pressure of demand in the economy with an eye on the regions of greatest labour shortage, then the total national unemployment will be greater the more the pressure of demand differs from one region to another. And the real costs of that, and to some extent of the *unevenness* of the distribution of the unemployment are, as we have seen more tangible.

Migration losses
Outward migration is the other aspect (or consequence) of poor economic opportunity in a region to which its inhabitants commonly object. Where those who go do so unwillingly, for lack of

25

local opportunities, their distress, and that of their friends and families, have an obvious basis. Not all do go unwillingly, by any means, though cases will vary widely. A fairly high proportion of people, especially the young, are positively attracted by the prospect of leaving home and seeing a different part of the world. But when the decline of local industries, for instance, throws people out of work with little chance of local re-employment, putting pressure upon them to move elsewhere, there is, of course, no guarantee that those subjected to this pressure are among the willing movers. Moreover, even the departure of willing emigrants from a region causes alarm and despondency to some other people in it, if it is not balanced by what they regard as an equivalent inflow. In all countries a considerable proportion of the employment in a region (in advanced countries nearly half of it) is generated by the demand of residents in that region. Reduction of the local population, or the outflow of potentially higher-earning members of it together with an inflow of people with lower purchasing power, is an obvious ground for alarm among all those whose livelihood depends on the local market. This alarm at any substantial emigration (or net emigration, at least) will spread to the local authorities and the local taxpayers. The alarm is not always wholly rational: losing people when economic opportunities are inadequate may mean reduction of the obligation to relieve poverty, and to provide services. It is not so much the net emigration as the shrinkage of employment opportunity lying behind it that is the legitimate object of complaint. But nobody – including local officials and politicians – likes to be concerned with the administration of a community that is in decline, even relative decline. The same applies in some degree when, as often happens, the younger and more mobile leave a community and are replaced by an inflow of the retired. People like to feel that they are on the winning side.

But, once again, from the point of view proper to a national government, what is the real cost of net emigration from one region? If it is migration out of the country, of course, it presents much the same (frequently exaggerated) grounds for objection at the national as at the regional level. If it is internal migration from one region of the country to another, the case is different. The distress of people whom the lack of local opportunity forces to move against their will, and who may not adapt quickly to new surroundings, still remains. But the alarm of local tradesmen or providers of services who see their opportunities shrinking in declining communities is matched, in this case, by the satisfaction of those who see their scope growing in expanding ones. And many of those who move may either do so willingly in the first place or, having moved with regret, may find more than adequate compensations later on – or, in the long term, their descendants may find a prosperity they would not have enjoyed in the ancestral surroundings. So far as the aggregate real income of the country is concerned, movement of people to areas of greater economic opportunity is likely to increase it in the long run.

There are two qualifications to this general presumption. Both of them are connected with limitations on the rate of shift of population that a country can stand without incurring penalties. First, if population in an area decreases, through net emigration to another region, faster than the social capital of the area – its houses, roads, schools and the like – falls due for replacement according to the criteria normally in use in the country, then there is an extra call upon national resources. Capital of these kinds has to be provided for the migrants somewhere else before that which they leave behind would, in the absence of movement, have had to be rebuilt. (If, as often happens, adequate capital is *not* provided in the areas to which they go, then they may pay a heavy penalty there in overcrowding and lack of amenities.)

Second, people living in communities have a limited capacity to accept social and economic change without developing antagonisms, or losing the established basis of their values and conduct, or both. This applies particularly to areas of rapid immigration, where old communities, which dislike some aspects of the change, come into conflict with immigrants, and the immigrants may find that they have lost the certainties (or at least the practical assumptions) of one way of life without having yet adopted those of another. The boom towns of the world have not been particularly civilised places, just as the declining areas have not been particularly cheerful ones.

Finally, among the considerations arising from inter-regional inequality of economic opportunity, one has to take account of the basically political fact that, inasmuch as regional communities are self-conscious, they (or rather, those that believe themselves to be at a disadvantage) resent and resist it.

It might be possible to show that the greatest growth of real national income would be promoted if all the economic development in a country took place in its richest region, large parts of the population of the other regions being transferred thither in

27

the process. But the people of the other regions, identifying themselves with their own regions, are likely to insist in such conditions that *they* should have a 'fair share' of the development, even
though that means having less development in total. This insist-
ence would be irrational if people were perfectly mobile within
the country: in fact, they are not, and they attach importance to
the persistence and prosperity of their regional communities,
even, in many cases, when they are themselves prepared to leave
them to seek their fortunes elsewhere. Thus, while it is true to
say that national policy ought to be concerned with the welfare
of people, not of regions as such, the attachment of people,
physically or emotionally, to regionally based communities sets
limits to the extent to which levels of economic opportunity in
different regions can be allowed to differ without endangering
national unity.

There is one final group of regional problems that to some
extent presents a less forbidding appearance than those we have
been discussing. There are cases in which the existing distribution
of population and industry, or the trend in it, gives concern to
the central government, quite apart from any complaint or
grievance in particular regions. Perhaps the clearest case arises
when the concern is basically strategic. In 1939, the Royal Commission on the Distribution of the Industrial Population (the
Barlow Commission) expressed the view that the concentration of
national resources in London was a strategic disadvantage. The
Soviet government's desire at various times to increase the proportion of industry and population east of the Urals clearly had a
strategic element. Sections of opinion in Norway, Sweden,
Finland and Australia have shown concern about the emptiness
of their respective northern areas, on the ground that it made
designs on them by a neighbour more likely to be conceived and
less easy to resist. Similar examples could be multiplied. While
the logic behind the initial apprehension is sometimes open to
challenge, the economic consequences that follow from it are
fairly straightforward, their interest lying chiefly in the thought
that has been provoked about the minimum size of settlement
that can provide sufficient amenities to hold its population in a
remote area.

There are somewhat similar non-military sources of concern.
In many countries, over a long period, townsmen have held views
about the desirability of preserving rural ways of life which not
all countrymen have shown convincing signs of sharing – hence

a considerable amount of the urban support for agricultural protectionism. The corresponding industrial romanticism of many developing countries may also command a following in rural as well as urban regions, but it still leaves plenty of room for inter-regional differences of opinion about where the industry that is so ardently desired should be located.

CHAPTER 2

Why Do Regional
Problems Exist?

EQUILIBRIUM WITH UNEQUAL GROWTH RATES

The argument of the last chapter brings one back to the question why there should be persistent and serious differences in economic opportunity between regions, if it is true that a proportionately small redistribution of labour, or capital, or both, would wipe these differences out. The first, and most important, part of the answer is that we are not dealing with a static situation that persists in remaining out of adjustment by what may be only quite a small amount. We are dealing with situations in which everything is changing (usually growing), and the *growth rates* are discordant. The simplest case, conceptually, is one where the growth rates of capital and labour – jobs and people of working age – are in step with each other in the country as a whole, but supply of labour by natural increase is ahead in one of the two regions into which the country is divided, while supply of jobs is ahead in the other. If this is so, unemployment will increase, and relative earnings will probably fall, in the regions where natural increase of population is running ahead; unfilled vacancies will pile up and relative earnings rise in the other region. This, however, will go on only up to a point. Migration of labour from the region where it is plentiful to that where it is scarce will tend to increase with every increase in the disparities of job opportunities and of pay. Soon it will reach the level at which it offsets the original disparity between growth rates of labour supply and of jobs. The levels of unemployment, unfilled vacancies, pay differences and migration will then all be stabilised, and may continue indefinitely.

A reasonable analogy is provided by two tanks of equal size, into which water flows at unequal rates. If the tanks are connected by a pipe, the difference in water level will build up to whatever is required to force water through the connecting pipe at a rate equal to the difference between the rates of inflow. If the pipe is narrow, the equilibrium difference in level will be large, if wide it will be small. In a similar way, the equilibrium difference of earnings and job opportunities between the two regions of our example depends on the reluctance of labour to move between them in response to these differences.

The economic mechanism is, of course, more complicated than we have so far admitted. One complication is that jobs, as well as people, are capable of moving. Disparities in the availability and price of labour will tend to divert new enterprise to regions where it is cheaper and more plentiful, so that there is a second adjusting mechanism, broadly like the first. Another consists in a gradual transformation of the structure of existing industry in the two regions towards specialisation upon, in the one case mostly labour-intensive industry, in the other case mostly capital-intensive, in response to the persistent difference in the relative supplies and prices of labour and capital. These extra channels of adjustment somewhat reduce the equilibrium differences in labour market conditions between the two regions, though it is doubtful whether, in the ordinary course of operation in response to market forces, they reduce it very much.

The whole of this theory of persistent inter-regional differences, however, only moves the burden of explanation back one stage. We have accounted for them in terms of persistent differences in growth rates of the indigenous supplies of factors of production; why should these differences, in turn, be persistent?

THE ROOTS OF INEQUALITY BETWEEN REGIONS

Demographic differences

We have to explain an appropriate amount of persistence in disparities both between regional rates of natural increase of population and regional rates of increase of jobs. So far as population is concerned, one might perhaps say that the onus is on anyone who wishes to prove that inter-regional differences in growth rate have any tendency to be either transitory or self-extinguishing. Natural increase of population depends upon so many factors – social, religious, technological and medical, as well as economic – that it might seem sensible for the economist to take it simply as a datum, which he is not required to explain. In extreme cases economic factors may be decisive, as when sheer starvation prohibits further increase, and there often seems to be a direct relation between year-to-year variations in prosperity and in birth rate. But, on the whole, natural increase of population does not adjust itself systematically to economic conditions; it manifestly depends, in ways that change only slowly, on numerous non-economic characteristics of a society. Rural communities, for instance, often show more rapid natural increase than urban ones, despite more limited immediate economic opportunities – a fact that contributes to one of the commonest kinds of inter-regional discrepancy in many countries. The nearest approach to a stabilising mechanism of natural-increase adjustment is probably that which operates through migration. The outward migrants from regions of low economic opportunity and high natural increase tend to be predominantly young adults, in the healthiest and most fertile years of their lives. Birth rates per thousand of the total population are therefore reduced, and death rates raised, in such areas, while opposite changes are produced by the cor-responding alteration in the age structure of total populations in the regions of greater opportunity, to which the migrants go. In the rather longer run, therefore, natural increase is not indepen-dent of migration, and thus of local economic opportunity (or lack of it), but changes in the inter-regional flow of migrants take some time to exert their full effects in this direction; what we are interested in is the natural increase of the population *of working age*, and a change in birth rate will not affect this for some years. In some cases, moreover, migration does not have the effects just described; in much of Africa, for instance, the flow of labour from the countryside to the towns is largely temporary and consists chiefly of men, who either return home to marry, or leave their wives and families at home in the first place. The association of high natural increase with poor opportunity can therefore persist for a long time and to a considerable extent, even where migration happens on a large scale.

What about adjustment through movement, or differential growth, of capital? On simple neo-classical economic principles, one would expect the rate of profit on capital to be highest where capital is scarce in relation to labour. That being so, and suppos-ing that capital is accumulated mainly out of profits, and has some tendency either to be ploughed back into the firms that make it, in the region where they make it, *or* (what will produce the same result in this case) to gravitate to the region where the return on it is highest, then a region that has surplus labour, because of a high rate of natural increase, should also soon acquire a high rate of growth of capital to set things right. Even without inter-regional mobility of capital, high profit rates where wages are low and competitive power therefore high ought to adjust the rate of increase of capital to that of labour. Why does this process so conspicuously fail to eliminate the kind of regional problem we have been considering?

There seem to be three main lines of explanation, which can be mentioned at once, though we shall have to return to them later also. First, it may be that, in generating regional problems, it is not so much disparities in the rate of growth of labour supply, but extraneous discrepancies in productivity of capital that are to blame – and we have noted that the forces bringing natural population growth into line with capital growth may be slow-acting, weak or non-existent. Disparities in the productivity (and growth rate) of capital may arise from many causes, but perhaps most obviously from the circumstance that the various regions specialise in different basic products, and demands for these products grow at different rates.

Second, the simple equilibrating mechanism may fail to work because, for some institutional reason, inter-regional wage differences do not arise to a sufficient extent to make the regions of labour surplus markedly more profitable than those of labour shortage. Third, it may be that our sketch of the simple equilibrating mechanism is still altogether too simple – that the productivity and accumulation of capital in a region depend not only on the extraneous influence of trends in demand for the basic industries' products, but also on some self-reinforcing tendencies. Through various channels which we shall have to consider later, success may feed upon success, or failure upon failure.

We have been looking at situations in which supplies of other factors of production are tending not to increase *pari passu* with the supply of labour in the various regions of a country, even though they are increasing with it in the country as a whole. More severe problems emerge if, even in the country as a whole, the supply of other factors of production is not keeping up (in some sense) with the supply of labour; this, of course, is the position in many of the poorer countries of the world. In particular, it often happens that, in the country as a whole, population increase is pressing on a limited supply of agricultural land, and that the supplies of capital and technical knowledge are not

33

adequate, even for the country as a whole, to make up for the increasing scarcity of land to such an extent as to yield satisfactory growth – or even maintenance – of the generally low prevailing levels of real income. If, in addition, the new economic opportunities created by investment (especially non-agricultural investment) are mostly in one region, there arises the form of regional problem that dominates the affairs of perhaps a majority of the countries of the world. The countryside supports a great weight of concealed unemployment, people whose absence would make very little difference to agricultural production. The more mobile of the surplus labour from the countryside moves into towns, where some of it forms a reserve, partly overtly unemployed, partly engaged in service occupations of very low productivity. The wages of those who gain regular employment (especially regular industrial employment), however, often remain much higher than incomes in the countryside, despite the reserve; their earnings are more likely to be protected by minimum wage legislation, or, to some extent, by trade union organisation and the scarcity of even the simplest industrial skills, or, in some cases, of basic literacy. Shortage of employment opportunities may be a problem of rural and urban regions alike, but the forms it takes are different, and the difference between the two in average incomes may remain wide.

Demand differences
But whether there is a shortage of jobs in the country as a whole or not, the question why it should be persistently worse in one region than in another is one to which we must return. We have so far considered only differences in the fertility of the population as a reason; another (perhaps more important) reason is difference in the rate of growth of demand for labour. To this we shall have to give rather more attention.

In the first place, it is useful to make the well-known (but sometimes misinterpreted) distinction between 'basic' and 'non-basic' (or local) employment. The latter is that which is engaged directly or indirectly in producing goods and services that necessarily end by being absorbed locally (or, in our context, regionally). House building, medical and other personal services, domestic electricty supply, retailing, are obvious examples. The employment that is usually quoted as most obviously 'basic' is that in the production of goods sold outside the region. Indirect as well as direct contributions must, of course, be counted. That part of employment in transport, for instance, that is attributable to producing goods for export from the region, or inputs into them, is 'basic', whereas that connected with local distribution of consumable goods, or local passenger transport, is not. But some employment in producing, directly or indirectly, goods that are in fact consumed locally must also count as 'basic'. Such employment may not be *essentially* local, since it may only yesterday have replaced employment in another region, from which our first region was previously supplied with these goods; or it may tomorrow disappear if goods produced in another region capture the local market. The criterion (inevitably not perfectly clear-cut, but nevertheless serviceable) is whether the *final* product to which the employment in question contributed, is effectively in competition with similar products made in other regions, or not; whether, to put it perhaps oversimply, the final product is *mobile*.

If we can assume that final expenditure is divided in a fairly constant proportion between mobile and immobile products, it follows that a more or less predictable amount of any increase in total employment in a region will consist of 'local' or 'non-basic' employment. Or, to put it in another way, any increase in 'basic' employment will carry with it a proportionate extra amount of local employment. The ratio of total additional employment (local plus basic) to additional basic is the ratio generally known as the 'basic employment multiplier'. The relevant point about it, for our present purpose, is that, so long as some roughly known value for it can be relied upon, growth of employment in a region may be said to depend solely upon growth of basic employment in it.

STRUCTURAL AND OTHER ADVANTAGES

Growth of basic employment in a region can usefully be approached by way of three questions: what are its basic industries? what is happening to employment in those industries in the country as a whole? are the region's industries gaining or losing in competition with the similarly classified activities in other regions? The first of these is a straightforward matter of fact, though the classification of industries that is used is of critical importance (which means that the available classification may be misleading). If the heads of classification lump together kinds of activity that are growing in employment, in the country, at very different rates, and which occur in different proportions to one

35

another in the country and the region, then the classification is a bad one for this purpose.

The second question (what is happening to employment in the relevant industries in the country as a whole?) is also straight-forward, if the classification we are using is appropriate. The point of asking it is that a region may have a high growth rate by virtue of having specialised on industries that are 'winners' in the simple sense that employment in them is growing fast every-where – in other regions as well as the one we are concerned with.

The third question – about competitiveness with other regions – is perhaps rather more complex in its implications. If all the region's industries are doing better, or all are doing worse, than the same industries in the country as a whole, we are led to ask further questions about the source of this general advantage or disadvantage. Does it spring from the favourable or unfavourable geographical location of the region (near to, or remote from, the main markets, for instance)? Or from a cultural tradition or social climate favourable or unfavourable to enterprise and innovation? Or from a technological change that makes its industries dependent upon the availability of some resource in which it is notably rich or notably deficient in comparison with other regions (like coal in the nineteenth century, for instance)? If inter-regional specialisation is very advanced, so that the region in question has basic industries that do not occur significantly in the rest of the country, the question about its competitive power in relation to them is, of course, meaningless. But where it has meaning, we are apt to find that the region does better than others in some basic industries, not so well in others. In that case, how well it is doing generally will depend on whether it happens to have specialised in the basic industries in which, on the whole, it does rather better than the rest of the country, or in those in which it does rather worse.

In short, then, a region may have a growth advantage over others for any of three immediate reasons: specialisation in industries that are doing well generally (presumably either because demand is shifting towards their products or because technology is advancing faster in them than in others); competi-tive advantage in all or most of its industries (presumably because of generally advantageous location, resources, or human and social attainments); and specialisation in the particular industries in which its physical and human endowments give it competitive advantage. More briefly still, it is a matter of structure, or competitive advantage, or a compound of the two. The proportions in which these three components are mixed varies from case to case. The coal-mining and traditional textile regions in the advanced Western countries have in the last generation or two mostly been suffering, and the manufacturing regions of the developing countries mostly gaining, from their structure. General competitive advantage is more easily illustrated at national than at regional levels – it is what Japan has; but, at least on a superficial view, it is exemplified by the Paris region within France, and Lombardy within Italy. The phenomenon of specialisation in the industry in which one does better than other regions was exemplified by the classical British textile regions (Lancashire and Yorkshire) in the nineteenth century (when they tended to drive other regions out of business in, respectively, the cotton and wool textile industries) and by the US southern states' capture of the textile industry from New England in the twentieth century.

But whether a tendency towards faster growth comes from fortunate specialisation, or from competitive superiority, or from a combination of the two, there are two important points to be noted about it. The first is that, if factors of production were not mobile between regions (as they are assumed not to be mobile between countries in the classical theory of international trade), this kind of advantage could, in principle, produce an indefinite divergence of standards of living. The second is that, because capital and labour, at least, are reasonably mobile between regions, what actually results is an indefinite tendency for the more fortunate region to continue to grow in population and capital at the expense of the less fortunate one.

Wages and profits increase in the more progressive community in relation to those in the other, and as they increase they draw in labour and capital at increasing rates. If there is nothing else to be taken into account, the region with the fastest growth will swallow up all the others – and at an increasing rate.

But generally there are other things to take into account. One is that productivity may depend on some factors that are not mobile between regions – natural resources in the widest sense, including space itself. These become scarcer in the region of rapid growth in relation to the rest of the country, and at some point the brake that this puts on the divergence of productivities may stabilise both the inter-regional differences in them and also the corresponding rate of flow of labour and capital to the faster growing region. This, however, may take a long time. Another possibility is probably more substantial in those cases where the source of superiority in one region's productivity growth is an improvement in the terms of trade between the products in which it specialises and other things. The possibility – probability, indeed – is that the improvement in the region's terms of trade will not last indefinitely. It can be checked in either of two ways. First, the shift of demand or of industrial technology that caused the improvement may cease, or be reversed after a time, or – what amounts to the same thing for the region in question – competing suppliers in other countries may be drawn into action. Second, the improvement in the terms of trade for the region's products is likely to stimulate production of them in other regions, which have hitherto not specialised in them so heavily, or have not produced them at all. Regional superiority based upon a wise or fortunate specialisation in industries that are doing well *everywhere* (or even in some other places that as yet do not specialise in them so heavily) is bound to diminish with time, because in all regions that possess the fastest growing industry, the regional rate of growth gets progressively nearer to that of the industry in question. The process, however, is bound, in most cases, to be interrupted before these regions all become specialised entirely in that industry. Otherwise we should find countries with only one industry – or perhaps more realistically only one basic industry – a state of affairs not often found.

'CUMULATIVE AND CIRCULAR CAUSATION'

Economies of scale
But in explaining the persistence over long periods of faster growth and higher incomes in one region than in others, there is another set of considerations to be taken into account – considerations connected with what Myrdal called 'cumulative and circular causation'. Perhaps we should distinguish two varieties of mechanism by which this can happen. The first consists simply in the existence of economies of large scale, and similar circumstances, working against the stability of the inter-regional distribution of activity. The second consists of ways by which the *rate* of growth of population or activity feeds back a positive influence upon its own level. Let us call them, for short, 'scale' and 'dynamic' mechanisms respectively. 'Scale' mechanisms are simple

enough in principle, however little we may know about them in practice. Just as it is well known that if, in a particular industry, firms become more efficient as they get bigger, the result is bound to be monopoly, so, if efficiency is prompted by big regional concentrations, either of one industry or of some complex of industries, or of industry and markets together, then there will be a tendency for bigger aggregations of the industry or industries concerned to grow faster than, or at the expense of, smaller ones. There is a simple physical analogy; the pressure inside a soap-bubble gets smaller the larger the bubble is. In any system of interconnected bubbles, therefore (e.g. if one tries to blow several bubbles at once from a pipe with several openings), the little ones will always empty into the big ones – only the largest bubble will in fact survive and grow.

Why there should be economies of scale at the regional level is a more complex question. The most obvious reason, familiar from the theory of competition between firms, is that efficiency is promoted by the division of labour between operational units, each performing a specialised function, and that the effective size of a single specialised unit of this kind is often large. There are other reasons arising from the advantages of 'pooling' or 'risk spreading' in various fields, and from the reduction of costs of distribution of consumable products. 'Efficiency', moreover, has to be interpreted widely in this context, as referring not only to the ratio of physical outputs to physical inputs in the production of goods and services, but to the ability to supply services and amenities in a large community, for the direct benefit of its inhabitants, that could not be provided in a small one – specialised entertainment, educational, health and other professional services, for instance, as well as the stimulus that many people derive from living in a large community in which much is happening, and the advantages that individuals and families derive from living in a place where there is a rich variety of employment opportunities.

Quantifying benefits of aggregation has proved to be an extremely difficult task. So has the quantification of the countervailing disadvantages that go with high density of population and industry in an urban complex – disadvantages of which traffic congestion, air pollution, lack of living space and the greater lack of countryside available for recreation are the most obvious. One thing that emerges very clearly, however, is that in the early stages of modern economic development in the country, the agglomerative power of these 'scale' economies is particularly strong. Sometimes the availability of productive public services - water, electricity, good transport connections with the outside world – is in this stage restricted to limited areas, often to the chief port or ports. Where the management of the 'modern sector' of the economy, public or private or both, is in the hands of either expatriates or a small indigenous class who, by education and interests, are separated from the rest of the population, the tendency of these people to congregate with their enterprises (so far as these are mobile) in a single region, usually the main port or capital region, is considerable. And once this has started to happen, this region comes to contain a high proportion, highly concentrated in space, of the country's purchasing power for manufactured consumable goods. Since an important part of early manufacturing development consists in substituting home-produced goods of these kinds for imports, the attraction that the overwhelmingly largest single internal market exerts over this development is very great. These tendencies, with varying relative strength, have shaped events in most of Africa and Latin America, and, indeed, in Australia, where the concentration of growth on the big cities, and especially (despite the great extent of the country) on the two very big ones, is particularly marked.

The gravitation of industrial and commercial development to a single region as industrialisation proceeds under modern conditions has been a great source of inter-regional friction. It has tended to mean a sharp geographical distinction not only between 'town' and 'country' – a dichotomy that has been important from the beginnings of civilisation – but also between regional standards of living; in the extreme cases a 'dual economy' in which the traditional ways of life of the one part were, in very large measures, untouched by the revolutionary changes proceeding in the other, and the economic interests of the two diverged sharply. In many instances political unity has been strained or ruptured in the process. In a country where town and country are mixed up together, their interests in matters of economic policy may still diverge sharply, and they often tend to support different political parties, but secession of either from the state that embraces them both is hardly practicable. Where 'town' is, in effect, all in one region, and 'country' in another, secession becomes a live issue. Strains of this kind have been important latterly in producing the alienation of Bangladesh from Pakistan. They were not unimportant, in the middle of last century, among the contributory causes of the American Civil War, nor, in this century, among those of the dissolution of the Central African Federation, and of the failure of an East African Federation to appear. If the economic forces tend to concentrate manufacturing industry into one region, and if manufacturing industry, the source of the most rapid growth of wealth, is subsidised (as it commonly is in these cases, through tariff protection) by the country as a whole, then some bitter rivalries are almost inevitable.

The peculiar strength of these forces in countries at early stages of industrial development is due to two main factors: the small size of the national market for any manufactured product in relation to the minimum economic size of plant for producing that product, and the absence of a nationwide 'infrastructure' of power, transport and other public services and, indeed, of pre-existing industry. In more highly developed countries with bigger total purchasing power, there is room for more than one – perhaps for many – of the establishments, or sets of linked establishments, that constitute the effective units of production in most manufacturing industries. The 'infrastructure' tends to be of more nearly uniform quality in all parts of the country or, at least, in a number of separate regional centres. Conditions of life available for managers and key workers, whose preferences play an active part, or have to be considered, in siting industry, are more nearly uniform between regions than in less developed countries. In 'old' industrial countries, too, there is generally a fairly wide scattering of industry inherited from days when local sources of power or materials, or local markets protected by relatively high transport costs, played bigger parts in determining its location – especially as the economies of large plant size were often not inherent in the technology of the time. This increases the number of nuclei on which new industry can crystallise, or the number of environments in which it can find adequate ancillary services, subcontractors and already skilled employees. This is not to say that the centralising tendencies due to economies of scale are absent in advanced countries; in France and Italy for instance (each of which has one strongly predominating industrial area) they are very important. But where manufacturing industry is starting from scratch, in modern conditions of technology, they are at their strongest.

There is one more important point to make about clustering together of population and industry under the influence of economies or other advantages of various kinds associated with large size of the cluster – it has in some circumstances a strong tendency to go too far, even leaving out of account the damage we have mentioned to national unity (assuming unity to be a virtue).

Beyond a point, every net addition to an urban aggregate's population will impose net burdens on the people already in it. In the short run, it will impose on them the burdens of congestion – that is to say, over-utilisation of (and consequently diminished quality of service from) the physical equipment of roads, public transport, water, electricity, sewerage, health, entertainment and educational facilities, and the trained manpower that goes with them – or a burden of building these facilities up to the larger scale now required. It will impose one or other of these burdens to an extent that, beyond a point, more than outweighs any advantage gained by having the existing facilities more fully utilised.

In the long run, when physical facilities and trained manpower have been adjusted to the demand for their services, there will still be a point beyond which more population means an increased burden on the community as a whole, largely through such factors as longer journeys to work and greater distance from the countryside, to an extent that is not compensated for by the various advantages that accrue from living in a bigger place.

The tendency will always be for the inflows and outflows of population to proceed according to the preferences of the people who move or choose not to move, preferences that take no account of the effects of the decisions upon the welfare of other people as a whole. The discomfort caused by the existing *level* of congestion or of excessive conurbation size is taken into account; the effect on other people of the *change* (or absence of change) of congestion or size following from one's decision to move or to stay is not. In any situation where a large aggregation is opposed to a great many much smaller communities, the result of this may well be that the aggregation grows more than is consistent with the maximum social advantage – taking account not only of the advantage to people who move, but also that of the populations they join and leave behind. In the short run there will tend to be excessive congestion in the aggregation. In the long run, even assuming that its facilities are able to catch up with demand for them, it will simply be too big.

Moreover, if the question is how many large urban 'clusters' the population and industry of a country is likely to crystallise into (leaving aside the probably continuing existence of a rural population, which is not crystallising into large clusters at all, though it feeds the urban clusters), then there is a possibility that a single cluster will form although the theoretical presumption is that there should be two of equal size. If the population destined to become urban lies in a certain size-range, probably somewhere between once and twice that which, in the absence of all other considerations, would provide the optimal real standard of living, then it is very likely that, of two clusters that may start to form, the larger will always present greater net attractions than the smaller, so that only one will in fact develop, although at the same time the social optimum would demand a division of the urban population between two clusters. Even if one looks only at possible positions of static equilibrium, there are various possibilities of divergence between what happens under everyone's search for the greatest private advantage and what is required for the greatest general advantage, and the bias seems to be towards excessive aggregation rather than the reverse.

Capital-stock adjustment

But let us pass on to the further possibilities that emerge when one considers the process of development during which the size and distribution of population and industry are not stationary, but are growing. The key to most of them is the existence of a positive relation between rate of growth and subsequent level of activity. The 'capital-stock adjustment' relationship is the most familiar specimen of this class, and the part it can play in the theories of growth and fluctuations is well known. As a short-term relationship – investment in an economy responding to changes in its rate of income growth in a matter of months – it is a staple of trade-cycle theory. The usual conclusion is that, if the accumulation of capital in a closed economy responded accurately and fully to changes in the prospective demand for it, as estimated simply from the rate of growth of demand for final goods and services as a whole, the level of activity would be wildly unstable – it takes a lot of investment to provide capacity for even a relatively small increase in the rate of output, and this investment, of course, would act powerfully to raise the demand for output subsequently. The resulting movement of activity might be cyclical or not (depending on, among other things, the time-lags involved), but one would certainly expect it to be violent

43

– either shooting sharply upwards, or downwards, or fluctuating with rapidly increasing amplitude.

In fact, it is pretty clear that the level of capital is adjusted to the level of activity and to population only roughly and over longish periods. We may therefore spare ourselves the trouble of considering the short-term instability of regional growth rates (in the present connection, at least), and start from the reasonable proposition that, over a decade, or a generation, the regions of a country with the more rapid rates of growth of population, employment and income might be expected to show the higher levels of per capita capital formation.

Suppose that one region is growing in population 1 per cent a year faster than the rest of the country. How much extra activity in the region is likely to be required to provide the capital for this steady extra rate of growth? Taking, for simplicity, only the employment effects, the answer depends on two things: how many man-years of investment activity are required to provide for one extra person in steady work? and how much of this extra investment activity will take place inside the region in question? The former of these is, in effect, the incremental capital-output ratio. It is a concept that may be formulated in several ways, but for this purpose we may take one of the simplest – the ratio of increments in gross capital formation to the accompanying increments in annual gross domestic product. Values of this ratio have been estimated by Beckerman for a number of countries in the period 1952–62, and by the United Nations both for some developed and some developing countries in the 1960s. They vary greatly, from less than two to nearly eight. If estimates were available for regions, the range of variation would no doubt be bigger, because the value obtained depends greatly upon the nature of the capital formation that is going on, and regions may be expected to show more variations in this respect than whole countries do. In the power industries, and in housing, the value is generally over ten; in transport often not much less. In manufacturing it varies between industries, but averages usually about three or four in the manufacturing sector as a whole. In mining, it tends to be a little bigger than this; in agriculture, variations of crop-yield make it more than usually difficult to estimate, but it probably varies with local circumstances and the type of agriculture (e.g. according to whether irrigation is one of the means of improvement concerned) from perhaps unity to five or more. A region well-endowed with agricultural land and climate that is

developing its agricultural production and some light manufacturing industry on the basis of a fairly adequate infrastructure of
transport and public buildings will probably have to invest the
equivalent of less than two man-years for each additional job it
creates. One that is developing hydro-electric power, extensive
irrigation, major transport networks and mining, smelting or
petrochemicals may have to invest the equivalent of eight or ten.

The second crucial question – how much of this investment
consists of activity actually in the region in question – will also
receive a variety of answers, according both to the nature of the
investment and to the industrial resources of the region. Generally, of course, information about imports of any kind into
regions is lacking, but some hints are given by the experience of
developing countries, many of them small, for which it is possible
to relate imports of capital goods to total gross domestic fixed
capital formation. This, however, will give an underestimate of
the imported content of the investment, inasmuch as raw or
semi-manufactured materials used in it, which are not classified
as capital goods, are omitted, and so are professional fees and
salaries paid abroad. United Nations estimates for 1960–2 and
1966–8 show ratios of capital goods imports to gross fixed
domestic capital formation varying between 5 per cent and 80
per cent, but averaging about 25 per cent. The inclusion of the
omitted items just mentioned might bring the average import
content up to something like a third, and for a region, as opposed
to even a small country, the corresponding figure would be higher
still.

Let us take an imaginary case where the capital-output ratio is
three and the proportion of the capital-forming activity that takes
place in the region is a half. Then our region where (as we
supposed earlier) population and employment are growing 1 per
cent a year faster than in the rest of the country will have capital
formation going on in it, at a rate equal to some 3 per cent of
its income more than would be the case if it were growing only
as fast as the other regions. Half of this extra capital formation
will involve employment in the region – something like 1·5 per
cent of the labour force will be engaged in it. But this extra
capital-forming activity in the region will generate another
addition to regional income through the ordinary muliplier
mechanism – the spending on regional resources of the extra
income that people in the region receive because investment is
higher. Given time for local services and the like to adjust to this

extra income, it might raise employment by another 1 or 1·5 per cent. A steady extra growth of 1 per cent a year in comparison with the rest of the country might therefore cause the *level* of regional employment to be 2·5 or 3 per cent higher than it would be without this extra rate of growth. There may well be complications here through the effects of the region's higher activity on other regions, and the repercussions of their consequentially higher demand on its activity. But the more important point to note is that our conclusion is reached by taking plausible middle values of our two variables (capital-output ratio and regional content of capital formation). Taking combinations of values of them that might well occur in practice, the additional regional employment attributable to an extra 1 per cent of growth might be anything from quite a small fraction of 1 per cent to something like 10 per cent.

This is not the place to go into the theory of stability and instability in rates of growth. Any consideration of it shows that the outcome of a change in a region's growth rate varies enormously according to the precise mechanism of interaction between the income multiplier and the adjustment of capital stock to income level that we suppose to exist, and the magnitude of time-lags in the working of the mechanism, which we are still far from being able to quantify. But one can say that, with the response of employment change to change in growth rate at the lower end of the range that has just been mentioned, stability would reign; a change in a region's growth rate would not tend to be self-reinforcing to any important extent. With the response near to the upper end of the very wide range that seems possible, on the other hand (that is to say, with capital-output ratio and regional content of capital-forming activity both high), one could reasonably expect tendencies towards instability. Any chance increase (say) in the rate of growth of one region in comparison with others would set up pressures to increase the gap still farther. The practical effect of this might be expected to depend largely on the mobility of capital and labour within the country (or from abroad, for that matter). If pressure of demand in a region is effective in drawing these factors of production in, then a regional boom can be self-reinforcing, at the expense of the rest of the country, to an important extent. Even if the mechanism is such as to reinforce regional booms only temporarily, it may still form a powerful mixture when combined with the tendency of one region to have a persistently superior growth rate for reasons of economic structure (i.e. because it has specialised more than others in industries of rising national or world demand) or with the effects of economies of large scale that operate at the regional level.

How important these dynamic tendencies are we simply do not know in general. An examination of the United Kingdom suggests that they have not recently been very important there. In a mature industrial economy with a relatively low rate of growth, replacement of capital is important in relation to its extension, and it so happens that the replacement of housing, and other social capital, mostly financed by the central government, has lately been faster in most of the old industrial regions of slower growth than in the more prosperous areas. The United Kingdom is also a highly integrated economy, within which the employment impact of capital formation in one region tends to fall to a large extent upon the others. Some writers on regional development in the United States have argued that mechanisms causing inter-regional differences of prosperity and growth to reinforce themselves cannot be very powerful there, either, because inter-regional differences have in fact shown a declining trend for a long time.

But if one thinks of an economy at an earlier stage of development, where a high proportion of capital formation in the most progressive regions consists of construction and public works, in which the capital-output ratio is high, and local labour makes a relatively large contribution, then it is by no means unlikely that these forms of 'cumulative and circular causation' augment the regional economies of scale that are in any case present at that stage, to a considerable extent. The only general inference is that different cases of regional growth differ from each other in the scope for the working of this kind of mechanism very widely indeed.

OTHER MECHANISMS OF SELF-REINFORCEMENT

It is worth mentioning another set of mechanisms of cumulative causation that is in essence simpler, though still very difficult to assess. Once a region acquires a faster rate of growth than others, the average age of its buildings and other structures tends to become lower than elsewhere, and so does the average age of its people – faster growth of population (if that is part of the picture) means either faster natural increase or more net immigration,

47

and both of these reduce the average age. (Net immigration does so because immigrants tend to be young adults, likely to start families.) Growing communities therefore acquire, in reasonably favourable circumstances, an association with newness and liveliness which may well help to draw other people and firms in. Regions of slow growth, or of declining population, become associated with the opposite qualities.

The other main member of this set of mechanisms operates through the machinery of public finance. In regions that become depressed the public authorities naturally suffer from declining, or only slowly growing, local revenues, but the claims on their resources may be unusually high, because of the relatively large incidence of poverty and unemployment. Their local taxation rates therefore tend to become higher than elsewhere, and the quality of the public service they can give lower, with the result that industry and those residents who can choose where to live (often the wealthier ones) will tend to go elsewhere, making the local depression worse. The working of this vicious circle is, of course, weakened where liability for dealing with poverty, unemployment and the local results of economic depression generally rests directly or indirectly upon the central government of the country rather than on local authorities. Centralisation of public finance in a country is one of the most powerful stabilisers of regional activity and development. It is worth noting, too, that whether it is centralised or not makes a great difference to the regional impact of migration. If the central government looks after the unemployed, depressed regional communities have an additional reason for deploring outward movements of their people in search of jobs (or better jobs) elsewhere, because this will decrease the number of unemployed in them, and the economic impact of national unemployment or relief funds on their economies will be lost. Communities that have to provide for their own unemployed, on the other hand, have every reason to play the old game of shifting paupers as quickly as possible into the next parish.

Finally, on this matter of cumulative tendencies, whether they come from economies of scale or from what we have called 'dynamic' factors, one should note why they concern the policy maker. They concern him because they are capable of distorting the geographical shape of the economy away from that which at any given time is 'optimal' – the shape that one would design for it if one was working on current information and was able to

48

bring the desired result into being instantaneously by some kind of magic. Naturally, since changes (as we have already noted) take a long time to make, the economy does not have this optimal form in any case; we are always burdened, or blessed, with what we have inherited from the past. But cumulative processes make us more the prisoners of the past than we should be without them. The great (often metropolitan) industrial aggregation is not necessarily where it 'ought' to be in view of today's technology and market opportunities; it is where the events of the past have assembled people and industry, perhaps in quite different technical and economic conditions, and have thus created economies of scale that still determine the optimal *marginal* movements of factors of production. To establish a rival to it (which may be desirable) is a large-scale operation, because the rival has to be big to be viable. Similarly, the boom area of today may owe some of its attractiveness and growth simply to the fact that it is in process of growing fast. To that extent, we finish up with population and industry, not where one would put them in the light of current natural resources and transport costs, nor even in the light of economies of scale derived from the accumulated legacy of the past, but disproportionately where the *rate of development* in some past period has created boom conditions.

How much does all this matter? The answer has to be framed in full consciousness of the fact, already mentioned, that one cannot, in practice, provide the alternative of perfect long-term planning, because the really long-term schemes of today will be obsolete before they can come to fruition. But anyone who travels in depressed regions (or, at least, in those where Myrdal's arguments are known) will face the contention that the region's day would surely come sometime, if only opportunities were not being pre-empted *now* by other regions on grounds that will not be relevant *then*. Sovereign states provide against this contingency, as well as they can, by various measures of protection and state enterprise. For the benefit of the government responsible for the relative fortunes of regions within one country, perhaps the best one can say is that market forces ought not to be regarded as sacred, but that the genuine importance of economies of scale in making possible development that would not happen without them (or would happen only at a considerable social cost in open or concealed subsidies) has to be taken seriously, while at the same time an administration that hopes to preside over the destinies of different communities with some measure of regional self-consciousness must not plan as if people and their local loyalties were more mobile than they are. If this ranks as a statement of the problem rather than a solution to it, it is not, on that account, to be regarded as without practical use.

Regional problems thus raise a good many points of economic theory, both static and dynamic, and they also raise a good many with which economic theory is not well equipped to deal. Many of them are, at least in part, political, in that they arise because people are attached to particular communities with a regional basis, or because central governments and those who support them attach importance to the preservation of states within which different regional communities exist. The motivations behind these attitudes are partly economic, partly non-economic, and the economic elements cannot be looked at in isolation without loss of reality. The main purpose of this book is to look at some particular instances of the most common and important kinds of regional problem that may be characterised as economic, with the qualification implicit in what has just been said, and to see what can be said about the main lines of policy that have been adopted for dealing with them. Before embarking on this task, however, it will be useful to sort out the main kinds of problem region – regions that give central governments economic grounds for concern.

CHAPTER 3

Types of Problem Region

In the foregoing chapters regional problems have been presented
as springing most frequently from immobilities of factors of
production, sometimes compounded by a shortage of job opportunities in the country as a whole. Very widely, it is possible to
view a country's regional problems as arising from a mislocation
of increase in job opportunities in relation to increase in population of working age, though the problem is somewhat different
– and more severe – if the rate of increase of job opportunities
is below that of population, taking all regions together. But
cultural, political and geographical peculiarities, as well as
economic ones, make every regional problem to some extent *sui
generis*. A first approach to greater realism can be made by
attempting a rough classification.

THE BACKWARD REGION IN DEVELOPING COUNTRIES

Most, perhaps three-quarters, of the world's population still lives
in what are called, with varying degrees of euphemism, the
'developing' countries. By this we mean countries in which by
far the greater part of the people are desperately poor, their
poverty generally being associated with some kind of farming
carried on by traditional methods, far removed from modern
techniques, and often in difficult climates, on difficult soils, and
with small amounts of land in relation to the numbers of people
trying to get a living from it. Yet in every country a substantial
part of total income is generated in what may be called, at least
by comparison, the 'modern' sector, by the activities of whole-
sale trade, whatever manufacturing industry there is (and there
is always some), the professions and the government. For reasons
that have already been touched upon, there is a very strong
tendency for these activities to be highly concentrated, often in a
single capital city. Incomes in the modern sector tend to be
relatively high; partly because productivity there, in physical

terms, may well compare much more favourably with that in corresponding activities elsewhere than does productivity in the traditional sector of the economy; party because, in an urban setting and under a wage system, trade union and other pressures make for the raising of wages, and the goods and services produced are in any case largely for a sheltered home market, whereas the traditional agricultural producer in the countryside is entirely at the mercy of his own meagre physical productivity and (sometimes) of the prices his products will fetch in world markets. There thus tends to be a sharp inter-regional – basically an urban/rural – division between living standards, which springs from a structural difference. The essential feature of the structural difference in this case, however, is that it is a difference between activities carried on largely with the benefit of modern knowledge and educational standards, and activities carried on by traditional methods, often without the benefit of modern technical knowledge, or even, perhaps, of literacy, and often under social systems that make for strong resistance to change.

The nature of the 'traditional sector' varies a great deal from one case to another. In all countries there is some production that is undertaken for immediate consumption by the producers and their families without ever coming to market, but in some there are large proportions of the population for whom production of this kind – 'subsistence production' – occupies most of their efforts and provides most of their consumption. There may now be no country where this subsistence production constitutes more than half the national product; relevant data are available for only a few developing countries, all of them in Africa; but since the income of a family in the subsistence sector, however assessed, is so much below average family income elsewhere in the economy, it may be taken that in a good many countries by far the greater part of the population still lives by traditional forms of production with very little recourse to the market. This is certainly so in Ethiopia and Malawi, for instance, where subsistence production was estimated in the sixties still to constitute more than 40 per cent of national product; it was probably true also of East Africa, where the ratio of subsistence production to the total was generally about a quarter. In these, and to a smaller extent many other developing countries, there are substantial proportions of the population, generally in the areas most remote from modern communications, whose manner of life connects them little with the rest of the country or the world.

These traditional subsistence economies within a country raise some of the most fundamental questions about development policy. First of all, should efforts be made to develop them at all? Traditional ways of life, which have proved their capacity to persist over very long periods, are apt to attract advocates of their retention and preservation. Views of this kind have had influence on the policies of some colonial and other governments: on the doctrine of 'indirect rule' in the British colonies in Africa, for instance, as well as, from time to time, on attitudes towards Indian tribal communities in the Americas.

But the decision is not a simple one. In the first place, traditional communities nearly always present some features that their scientifically more advanced neighbours are generally unwilling (or perhaps in the longer run unable) to leave alone – notably high levels of mortality, which relatively simple hygienic and medical changes will reduce. Once this is done, the balance between the traditional community and its environment is upset, and the preservation of its way of life becomes impossible. Game is exterminated, pasture land overgrazed, cultivable land becomes scarce in relation to population or deteriorates in quality. Moreover, even without an increase of population pressure, the attractions of a higher material level of life are apt to draw the more enterprising from the traditional into the modern sector. An accommodation is possible, and is very widely achieved in Africa, for instance, by which young men go to work for a time in the mines or factories of the modern sector and then return. (The same thing happens, of course, with the temporary migration of Irish workers to Great Britain, of Turks and Yugoslavs to Germany, and formerly happened on a large scale with temporary migration from eastern and southern Europe to the United States.) But returned emigrants do not fit readily into the original framework of tribal societies; they bring new ambitions and new material wants with them. These influences may also hasten permanent emigration. In one way and another, societies at lower income-levels are radically changed by contact with those at higher levels, even if they can be saved from exploitation by the latter – which is not always easy.

Regions in which the economy is largely a subsistence one have in the past coexisted with modern-sector regions for long periods, though changing slowly all the time; but the pace of change has quickened, and it is doubtful whether true subsistence sectors of any considerable size will remain anywhere in the

53

world a generation hence, even in the absence of national policies aimed at bringing them into the market economy. Such policies will, of course, be attempted (as they are attempted now), partly because the existence of a subsistence sector is thought in some quarters to constitute a challenge, partly because its disorderly break-up (in the way that has been outlined) gives rise to demands from it for some positive action, and partly because the too-rapid flow of emigrants from it into the modern sector presents problems there – a point to which we shall have to return.

The subsistence sector, however, is an extreme case. In most countries a large part of the countryside is occupied by small agricultural (or sometimes pastoral) producers who have been in some considerable degree drawn into the market economy; they produce crops or animal products to sell. Their life is less out of touch with the modern sector than that of subsistence producers under a tribal regime, but there are very few countries where their average incomes are not far below those of the city-dweller – very commonly they may be only a half or a third of the latter. In most cases their situation is complicated by a high rate of natural increase and an absence of readily available extra land on to which to expand. It is common to find in developing countries a rate of natural increase of population of something like 2·5 per cent a year. This brings a doubling in not much more than a generation; those coming to be of working age now are nearly twice as numerous as those of their parents' generation at the same age. The pressure to find more land (which is often not available), more output per acre, or more jobs off the land, is intense. To accommodate in the non-agricultural sector of the economy the whole of the natural increase in such cases would require a very high rate of investment. A United Nations calculation implies that, in the majority of the developing countries, to employ in industry (even without any increase in the non-industrial infrastructure that would certainly be required) the whole of the increase in the population of working age, with the level of capital equipment per industrial worker now ruling in these countries, would take something like twice the present national levels of net investment. This at least serves to indicate that the growth of rural population (which is most of the total population-growth in these countries) presents problems. These problems are not insoluble, but they may be taken as general evidence that central governments, often physically insulated in their capitals from the countryside, have some reason to think about rural matters.

In any case, rural regions, whether in developing countries or anywhere else, are apt to give central governments notice of their existence, if they have a voice at all. Apart from the tendency for agricultural incomes to be relatively low, there is the risk of crop failures, to which is added, in the case of commercial agriculture, the risk of price depression in world markets. Both of these risks are greater where there is a high concentration on one product for the world market, as is very commonly the case in the developing countries of the tropics, with their concentration on, for instance, coffee, cocoa, sugar, cotton or rubber. Either risk is apt to produce a crisis that cannot be ignored.

Where the regions in question also produce largely for export (and this is true of mineral-producing as well as agricultural regions), a classic conflict of interest is apt to arise with the region or regions (most often the metropolitan region) of the modern sector. The latter commonly contain the incipient manufacturing industries, nearly always protected by tariffs, so that the prices of their products to the exporting regions are raised. It is harder for corresponding benefits to be given to the exporting regions; only subsidies would help, and tax revenue for providing subsidies is generally scarce. There is, at least, an inter-regional conflict of interest on such basic policy questions as protection and the external value of the currency.

To summarise, then, a true subsistence region in an economy presents all the problems of developing a technically primitive economy, and in the long run leaving it alone is not practicable. A primary producing region selling in the world market is apt to have policy interests that conflict with those of the manufacturing (generally the metropolitan) region, and, like a subsistence region, to present development problems because of rapid population increase, as well as suffering from year-to-year instability of its income.

The kinds of policy that are called for will vary. In subsistence regions, the gradual improvement of agricultural techniques may be the first priority, but with this is likely to go the introduction of some production for the market, and this in turn is likely to demand extensive improvement of transport and communications. In the primary producing region that has already reached the stage of producing for the market, some means of transport will normally have been developed, but further improvement, coupled with improvement of production techniques, may well be high on the list of priorities. Beyond this, however, there are likely to be demands for measures to stabilise agricultural incomes, and, at some stage, for a decentralisation of industrial development, so that the benefits of the higher industrial incomes and of industrial protection, may be more evenly shared between regions, and the need for the more enterprising people from the primary producing areas to leave their regions in search of work may be reduced. Needless to say, these demands are likely to be the more insistent the greater the cultural differences between regions.

THE BACKWARD REGION IN MORE DEVELOPED COUNTRIES

So far, we have been concerned with developing countries, the regional problems of which we shall not explore further in later chapters. More highly developed countries have problem areas not dissimilar from some of those just discussed. Such remnants of subsistence regions as they have are, of course, vestigial and mostly of less than regional size – the Indian reservations of the United States are perhaps the best examples – but they do in many cases still have extensive regions relying mainly upon small-scale agriculture, which present problems not unlike those found in developing countries. We shall look more closely at some of these regions later. For the time being it may suffice to note that they differ from their developing country counterparts mainly in that the neighbouring modern-sector regions are generally much larger and better able to absorb manpower, their contacts with them better developed, and their own rates of natural increase of population are lower. In consequence, whereas a surplus of manpower on the land tends to exist in developing countries, despite very heavy emigration to cities, in the more highly developed countries manpower leaves the land at rates that may lead to a sense of shortage.

MINERAL-PRODUCING REGIONS

Some reference has already been made to mineral-producing regions. In the developing countries, these are generally areas of relatively high income, often exporting substantial parts of their products abroad. They are then subject (as we have noted already) to the uncertainties of world market conditions and, as anywhere else, mineral deposits may be worked out; but in developing countries poverty and insecurity are not (at least by comparison with other regions) the marks of these areas. Rather it is their difference of interest from other regions that is a source of difficulty. Their inhabitants tend to believe that they would be better off in a state of independence, both from manufacturing regions which they are called upon to subsidise by purchasing their high-cost, protected goods, and from the poorer agricultural regions whose development and services they are called upon to support through taxation in general. The attempt in the early sixties of the copper-mining province of Katanga to escape from political incorporation in the Congo (now Zaire) is a case in point; so (though other issues were also involved) was the attitude of the neighbouring Northern Rhodesian copper belt to the former Central African Federation of which it formed part.

In more advanced economies, mineral-producing regions have more often presented problems for other reasons; not so much because they are prosperous and resent sharing their prosperity (though that may happen in Scotland as she becomes a substantial oil producer) as because, through the exhaustion or the supersession on the market of their mineral products, they lose their chief means of livelihood. There are plenty of 'ghost towns' that once flourished on the mining of some mineral and, with the exhaustion of their deposits, or changes in the market, have been almost, or entirely, deserted. There are also plenty of cases in which mining operations on a considerable scale were once superimposed on the other activities of a rural community, but have vanished, leaving little trace of their existence except abandoned workings – this is true, for instance, of lead mining in the English Pennines.

The most important feature of mineral extraction, from our point of view, is, perhaps, that it is apt to be done in out-of-the-way places. Many minerals have a positive tendency to occur in mountainous regions, which are usually both difficult of access and not agriculturally attractive, so that (apart from mining communities) they are thinly populated. Even if the distribution of workable minerals were purely random with regard to space, it would still be in some sense remote, because the distribution of population and economic activity over the world is very highly localised. One would expect minerals to be correlated with economic activity only insofar as the minerals are the cause of the location of the activity. In fact, the employment involved in the extraction of most minerals is not so great as to require major concentrations of population in the neighbourhood of the work-

57

ings. The most important historic case where it does is, of course, coal, mostly because coal is produced in very large quantities; though even there, 'concentration' is perhaps the wrong word – it is characteristic of coalfields that, though the mining and associated populations on them may be large, they tend to be scattered over considerable areas in mining villages and small towns rather than brought together in large cities or conurbations. The number of people involved, on the spot, in extracting petroleum is now also large. Perhaps the more important consideration, however, is how far the locations of mineral deposits attract activities other than their extraction and immediate processing. Historically, coal has been a great attracter; the more so where deposits were not close to tidewater (and hence to cheap transport), and, within the last 200 years, the more so where development was early – before cheap transport, and before the more efficient use of coal to provide larger quantities of energy per ton. The increasing use of energy in the form of electricity has, of course, tended to weaken the pull of the coalfields.

As for oil, a large part of its competitive advantage against coal consists precisely in its easier transportability. Its tendency to attract industrial activity to the places where it is extracted has, consequently, been slight. The attractiveness to employment of the places where it is refined is greater; not because refining itself provides much employment – it is one of the most highly capital-intensive of all industries and its employment is relatively very small – but because of the growth of the petrochemical industry dependent upon refinery by-products. Despite the very rapid growth of this industry, however, the tendency to form large industrial complexes based upon it is not particularly strong; the industry produces materials which are themselves mostly transportable at low cost in relation to their value, and they move readily to the numerous and varied manufacturing industries in which they are used.

The only other mineral that is used in such large quantities as to exercise a considerable effect on the location of economic activity as a whole is iron ore – again, not because of the employment in the mining of it, which is small, but because of its influence on the iron and steel industry. But this is an increasingly diffuse influence; any site that is readily accessible to very large ships will do, and the picture is further blurred by the extent to which steel making depends on scrap as a material, and hence upon accessibility to the main areas where metal goods are used.

The upshot of all this, for the present purpose, is that, apart from the coalfields that developed early as major centres of industry and population, mineral-producing areas do, indeed, have a fairly strong tendency to be, and to remain, remote from concentrations of other kinds of economic activity; hence they are, of all the broad classes of problem area, perhaps the most likely to suffer absolute decline when circumstances turn against them.

MANUFACTURING REGIONS

Manufacturing regions present a somewhat different set of problems when, for reasons of technology or markets, the growth of demand for labour in their industries falls persistently short of the natural increase in their workforce. In the first place, it is generally a more modern problem. It is true that some manufacturing areas have lost their basic industry in circumstances that produced an effect rather similar to that of a collapse of mining activity – a degree of reversion to a basically rural structure. This happened, for instance in the eighteenth century and earlier, as the very many small ironworks in Britain and elsewhere, that relied on local supplies of timber for charcoal smelting, exhausted those supplies. It is doubtful, however, whether this activity was (in Britain, at least) ever the major activity of any area of truly regional size. There are also numerous cases throughout the world of the extinction of handicrafts, as factory-made goods (in many cases imported) have come upon the scene, but there again, the lost activities, though their loss caused hardship, were generally subsidiary to a basically agricultural way of life – at least if assessed on the regional (as opposed to a smaller, local) scale. Something nearer to the problem of the modern depressed industrial area can perhaps be seen in the collapse of the East Anglian wool textile industry in the early nineteenth century, under pressure of competition from the West Riding of Yorkshire, where availability of power was apparently the main component of a combination of circumstances giving superiority. East Anglia became, at any rate, the only English standard region ever actually to decline in population over a decade, since censuses began at the outset of the nineteenth century. But the modern, large-scale phenomenon of the persistently depressed manufacturing region naturally did not arise until predominantly

59

manufacturing regions had not only come into existence, but had also in some cases grown old. The first regions to specialise in the oldest of factory industries – textiles – are not surprisingly among the most conspicuous examples, and some of them will have to be considered in a later chapter.

The second characteristic of the depressed manufacturing regions may be regarded as a result partly of their relative modernity, partly of the peculiar blend of similarity and diversity among manufacturing industries. From their relative modernity, it follows that manufacturing regions do not lack a serviceable infrastructure of roads, railways and urban amenities, as agricultural and also to some extent mining areas often do. From the similarity in the requirements of many different manufacturing industries – a workforce that is at least literate, and preferably accustomed to going out to work, factory space provided with public utility services and good communications – there arises the presumption that once an area has specialised in some kind or kinds of manufacturing industry, there is a high probability that it will be reasonably attractive to some other varieties. It is also broadly true that manufacturing areas, unlike some mining areas, have not developed in inaccessible places. If they have developed at all, then, even though their original basis for prosperity may have vanished, there is a reasonable probability that they will not be seriously handicapped by their location in their efforts to develop new manufacturing activities. In short, *a priori*, the prospects of regeneration of manufacturing areas that have fallen on bad times should be reasonably good.

There are some obvious qualifications to this general proposition. One of the most important is that any industrial region that has run through the life cycles of one or more manufacturing specialisms is likely to suffer from an infrastructure, 'a built environment', that is to some extent run-down and unattractive. Some industries in decay are especially apt to leave large areas of dereliction, notably the heavy industries – though mining is generally a worse offender in this connection. Again, some manufacturing areas establish traditions of stormy industrial relations – particularly in their days of adversity and shrinking employment opportunities – which hinder the generation or introduction of new industry. Moreover, the requirements of some industries for factory space are very specific. When they start they cannot take over existing accommodation built for other kinds of industry, and when they close down, their buildings are an embarrassment rather than an asset to some other kinds of industry that might want to come in. The balance of these advantages and disadvantages is clearly central to an appreciation of the problems of depressed manufacturing regions. At all events, these problems are, *prima facie*, different in important respects from those of either agricultural or mining regions in difficulties.

'CONGESTED' REGIONS IN DEVELOPING COUNTRIES

Finally, we come to the quite different kinds of problem regions – those at the receiving end of the flow of labour. The natural presumption from our earlier simple theoretical discussion might be that all such regions suffer from shortage of labour rather than unemployment, and that their main problems might be those of 'excessive' development, as seen by the people of other regions, or the central government; or problems connected with 'congestion' in some sense. It is not, however, so simple as that in practice. In the first place, there is a class of problem region – arguably, taken together, the most alarming problem regions in the world – where heavy inward migration goes with heavy unemployment and underemployment. These are the major city regions (usually metropolitan) of, principally though not exclusively, the developing countries. They differ from, say, the regions containing modern Turin or Milan or Brussels, which are the most important magnets of internal migration in Italy and Belgium, in that they are areas of heavy unemployment and underemployment. They tend to attract people more rapidly than they can provide employment for them. They also draw them in more rapidly than they can provide for them in other ways; their populations tend to be greatly excessive in relation to their infrastructure. This state of affairs constitutes congestion in the most literal and general sense – pressure on the physical and administrative equipment of the area beyond its capacity for coping with it.

The scale of the congestion problem in this sense is enormous. In the countries classified by the United Nations as 'developing', the aggregate growth rate of population is about 2·5 per cent a year, but the rate of growth of urban populations (defined as those in locations of more than 20,000 inhabitants) is between 5 and 6 per cent. There is, however, a tendency for growth to be fastest in the biggest aggregations. About half the approximately 150 urban aggregations of more than a million people in the world are in what must be classified as poor and still mainly agricultural countries (a classification wider than the United Nations' 'developing countries', which do not, for instance, include China). The annual growth rates of many of them are probably in the region of 7 per cent (i.e. they double in a decade) and some considerably higher. This is an aspect of the concentration of growth in a developing country on a single urban centre, or a small number of such centres, to which reference has already been made. It is not confined to poor countries; it is, rather, an aspect of *modern* growth in a country not industrialised earlier, as witness the concentration on a small number of large centres in Australia and the wealthier Latin American countries, as well as in the poorer ones.

The degree to which this development has outrun the provision of permanent housing, not to mention other urban amenities, can be judged from the fact that, in the large cities of the developing countries taken as a whole, probably a quarter or a third of the inhabitants are squatters, living in shanties or similar dwellings built by themselves, usually in defiance of both planning and sanitary regulations (if there are any). In more than half the developing countries (UN definition) for which data were available, the proportion of urban houses with flush toilets in the early sixties was below 50 per cent; the coverage of these statistics was almost certainly such as to give an unduly favourable impression in relation to the true general position. It is true that the state of rural housing, judged by presence or absence of services, is probably little, if any, better than that of the shantytowns (it is certainly worse than that of the towns taken as a whole), and that many of these developments are in relatively kind climates; but the urban concentration of squalor, combined with the fact that the people concerned are not only poor but economically insecure and removed from their familiar surroundings, makes for social and hygienic problems of horrifying dimensions.

'CONGESTED' REGIONS IN DEVELOPED COUNTRIES

The rapidly developing region that draws people in faster than they can be provided with employment is not confined to the developing countries, nor is it exclusively a modern phenomenon. London before 1914 showed the highest rates of trade union unemployment in Great Britain: a reflection, probably, of its power to attract people in hope of finding employment, especially at a time when the decline of agricultural employment in the neighbouring parts of the south of England, and elsewhere, was fairly rapid – though our knowledge of the situation, and especially of agricultural unemployment, is incomplete. The picture since 1918, with London unemployment rates consistently among the lowest, is at least superficially very different.

The British region now of fastest growth and highest inward migration, the south-west, does not show one of the lowest unemployment rates; though this has probably less to do with the immigration into it than with the seasonal nature of some of its more traditional industries. Its unemployment rate is not one of the highest either.

In the United States some of the regions of rapid growth by immigration from the rest of the country show unemployment rates well above the national average. This is true generally of the Pacific and mountain states, especially California, though the highest rates, in general, are found in depressed regions. France, also, seems to show some association between rapid growth (and high inward migration) and high unemployment. The unemployment rate in Paris is above the national average, though not high; those in the rapidly growing regions of the Mediterranean coast, however, are the highest in the country. Some of the areas of rapid growth in Germany, also (Bremen and Cologne, for instance), show higher than average unemployment, though the absolute rates have until recently been very low.

That high unemployment and high inward migration should go together is, of course, by no means inexplicable; it suggests that the migrants are moved by something other than a better chance of simply getting a job in their region of destination – the possibility of getting a better-paid job, for instance. This is an important consideration in many cases, including both the developing countries and most of the developed ones, where the sources of the migration are mostly agricultural regions, with average incomes per head often very low compared with those in urban areas. In many cases, too, the attractiveness of urban life, at any rate in prospect, may be regarded as a powerful motive, independent of employment prospects or pay. Moreover, the low level of unemployment rates in rural regions may give a false impression; it is often the case, not that there is no surplus manpower there, but that there is underemployment – more people on family farms, for instance, than are needed to work them – or that many people can make a poor living on smallholdings and, for administrative reasons or because of lack of local opportunities, they do not appear on a register of unemployed. Differences in methods of recording may be largely responsible for the fact that, whereas (as we have noted) France shows the highest unemployment rates in some areas of heavy inward migration, Italy shows a strong negative correlation between regional unemployment rates and regional gains by migration – so in general do Belgium, the Netherlands and Denmark.

But whatever the anomalies and statistical ambiguities shown by comparisons of urban and rural unemployment rates, the important distinction for our present purpose is between those growing urban regions where unemployment and underemployment are high and those where they are low. In the former, there is the manifest evil of involuntary idleness and consequent poverty; in the latter there is not. In both there may be inadequacy of social provision – housing and the like – though in the nature of things this is likely to be (and is) much worse where the urban region cannot supply adequate capital to provide employment either; it is predominantly a feature of the developing countries, though in the developed ones housing shortage, absolutely much less severe in general, naturally tends to be *relatively* greater in the growing regions.

The rapidly growing regions where unemployment is low might seem to give little ground for concern, unless it is, indeed, the case that their social (as opposed to their industrial and commercial) infrastructure is lagging behind the need for it. It is true that they often excite resentment in other regions – a matter which policy makers cannot altogether dismiss by putting it down to simple jealousy. But even apart from such considerations of inter-regional equity and national unity, there are possible grounds for concern connected with 'too much' of the national growth taking place in one, or a small number of, regions. It has already been noted in an earlier chapter that there is at least a theoretical possibility that major concentrations of people and industry, even when adequately serviced, may have a tendency to grow too big for the optimal welfare of the country as a whole, and may call for intervention to modify the pattern. But it is perhaps generally more to the point that their services, especially their transport arrangements, tend to become inadequate through technical change and the sheer process of their growth; what was adequate for the urban area when it was smaller, and before the invention of the motor-car, and would still be adequate in smaller aggregations, leaves a problem of congestion in the larger aggregation today. Rapid growth of the areas of the big urban complexes, moreover, may produce both an increased separation of people from their job opportunities (which, for the poor, may be serious to the point of disaster), and a mismatch between the taxable capacity and the financial needs of local governments within the conurbations. Problems of these kinds may increase in seriousness with size – not only absolutely but in proportion to the numbers of people affected – though the issues are complex ones, to which we shall have to return in a later chapter. At all events, even prosperous regions with high growth rates present problems that bear upon national policy for the broad location of industry and population.

This survey of different types of problem region has inevitably been both brief and incomplete. Every case is different from every other one, and any classification begs questions; but some classification is necessary if anything useful is to be said at all. From the broad, though sketchy, view so far presented, we shall now turn to more detailed surveys of some of the types of problem region which we have been attempting to distinguish, basing them on selected cases for which reasonably adequate data are available.

CHAPTER 4

Agricultural Problem Regions

WORLD AGRICULTURAL TRENDS

Agriculture still occupies something like half of the economically active population of the world, though the proportion varies nationally – and still more regionally – from less than 2 per cent at one extreme to 80 or more per cent at the other. At the same time, despite growing population and, in most countries, growing per capita income, demand for agricultural produce in general is increasing very much less fast than demand for non-agricultural goods and services. This can be attributed to two kinds of influence. On one hand, the growth of technical knowledge leads to the substitution of non-agricultural for agricultural materials – most obviously synthetic fibres for cotton, silk and wool, synthetic for natural rubber and, synthetic plastics for leather. On the other hand, as per capita incomes rise, the proportion of them spent on foodstuffs tends to fall. This happens to different extents at different income levels; in relatively poor countries the income elasticity of demand for foodstuffs (the ratio of percentage rise in per capita food consumption to percentage rise in per capita income) can be quite high, but in all the advanced industrial countries it is low, and the figure for the world as a whole is well below unity.

The balance of production is thus shifting away from agricultural products. The implications of this for farm activity vary widely. In many countries where agriculture is largely on a subsistence basis, or is traditional in its methods, the productivity of labour in it has risen little, whereas productivity in the industrialised sector of the economy has risen relatively fast. In these circumstances, agriculture has kept its share of the total active population, and its problem has tended to be one of decreasing relative incomes, a tendency sometimes exacerbated by land shortage in the face of rising population. In the advanced countries, in contrast, the productivity of labour in agriculture has been rising fast. In all West European countries (and in the USA) it has been rising in the last twenty years faster than the corresponding figure of productivity per person occupied in the non-agricultural sectors as a whole. The effect, reinforcing that of the relative shift of demand away from agricultural products, has been to diminish the relative demand for agricultural labour at a very rapid rate. In the twenty-two years 1950–72, the numbers engaged in agriculture in northern and central Europe fell by more than 50 per cent; in the southern countries of the continent, where the proportion so engaged started much higher (round about half the total, as compared with something like a quarter in the centre and north), the numbers fell by about a quarter. Altogether the number engaged in agriculture in Western Europe fell by some 16 million. The agricultural labour force of the United States fell in the same period by between 3 and 4 million.

Part of the drift from the land over a long period has been caused, and the relative standards of living in agricultural and non-agricultural regions have been modified, by a broad movement of the terms of trade against agriculture in the world as a whole. This has affected most directly the agricultural exporting countries; elsewhere measures of agricultural protection and subsidisation have cushioned or cancelled its effect, and where agricultural productivity has risen fastest, relative incomes have been maintained in spite of falling relative prices. As a general world tendency, however, one can see over the twenty years up to 1972, taken as a whole, a relative cheapening of agricultural products and a fairly widespread relative worsening of agricultural incomes. Indeed, the same is true of a much longer period, of perhaps a century, interrupted only by the two World Wars. The great relative rise of agricultural prices in 1972–3 may change this for the future, but it cannot reverse what has already happened. In any case, in most countries of the world (Australia and New Zealand being, as is well known, the outstanding exceptions), average incomes and agriculture have long been below those in the non-agricultural sectors. This can be seen as an example of the effect of friction in a changing situation, which we have put forward in an earlier chapter as a central feature of regional problems. The shifts of demand and technology have, over a very long period, been tending to move factors of production from agricultural to non-agricultural employment. The movement is, in general, resisted. The majority of people cling to the means of earning a living with which they are brought up. In the case of agriculture, the surroundings, the social setting, the whole way of life, are widely different from the mainly urban conditions in which most non-agricultural activities take place, and to some extent those who are brought up with them either prefer them, or are unwilling to venture into a different and largely unknown environment, or, if they do so venture, may find themselves ill-equipped for it. Generally speaking, therefore, throughout the world, there tends to be an income differential in favour of non-agricultural activities which is sufficient to move agricultural populations into them, at a rate which, given constant speeds of movement in demand and technology, and constant rates of natural increase of population, would settle down to being a constant one. If the rate of change of demand and technology in favour of non-agricultural labour increases, then the expectation is that the rate of change of the structure of employment will, after a period of adjustment, change correspondingly, and that the income differential against agriculture will increase also.

This tends to be true of the world as a whole, so far as one can generalise about it; it is also broadly true of the national economies within it that are most nearly self-sufficient. The pattern of events varies greatly, however, from one country to another, because agriculture and industry are protected from world market forces to very different extents in different countries and, partly as a result of this, relative rates of increase in productivity in agriculture and in industry vary widely. So do the degrees of mobility of labour between agricultural and non-agricultural occupations. In the most highly industrialised countries agriculture is everywhere fairly heavily protected and, as already mentioned, agricultural productivity has been increasing rapidly, thus keeping up relative incomes. But because these countries are highly urbanised, education is widely diffused, and the advantages of urban life, and of non-agricultural employment, are familiar to nearly everybody, the drift from the land is relatively rapid. There is often little agricultural unemployment, either open or concealed; rather there is often complaint of a shortage of agricultural labour as people move from agricultural areas, though this is not sufficient to force agricultural wages up to the industrial level. The problems are those that arise from rural depopulation. The more highly urbanised the country is already, and the more closely integrated town and country are in a general, cultural sense, the less are the strictly economic hardships that this causes.

Recent trends in the United Kingdom illustrate this. The general background, over the decade of the 1960s, for instance, is that total physical production in agriculture rose nearly as much proportionately as that in the rest of the economy (in round figures, by 25 per cent, against 30 per cent elsewhere), but whereas the number of people engaged in non-agricultural activities increased slightly (by about 3 per cent) that in agriculture fell (by nearly 30 per cent). Physical output per person directly engaged rose more than twice as much in agriculture as in the rest of the economy – some 58 per cent against 27. The relative price per unit of agricultural output fell; the consumer got most of the advantage of relative increase in productivity. Income per person engaged in agriculture seems to have risen a little relative to the average for the whole economy, but the relative gain was concentrated on the self-employed – employees maintained their average income at just about a constant proportion (80 per cent) of the national average. Their numbers fell sharply, by some 38 per cent, which was probably about twice as great, proportionally, as the fall in the numbers of the self-employed.

The United Kingdom has no agricultural regions, in the sense of major (or 'standard') regions in which agriculture occupies the majority of the occupied population – or even the majority of that part of the occupied population (generally half, or a little more) that is not engaged in providing essentially local services. The regions that depend most on agriculture are East Anglia, with 9 per cent of its occupied population in agriculture, and Northern Ireland, with 8 per cent. This means that, whatever happens to agriculture, it cannot exercise a dominant influence on a regional economy, though in the two regions just mentioned, as well as (though to a smaller extent) in Scotland, Wales, the north and, the south-west, the decline in agriculture's demand for labour has been a far from negligible factor. It is only at the sub-regional level that agriculture is sufficiently important for its fortunes to dominate.

In England and Wales, moreover, the essentially rural areas, with relatively high proportions of their occupied populations in agriculture, do not form very large continuous tracts. The East

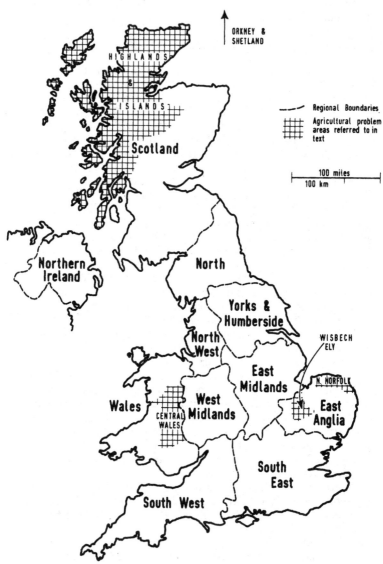

United Kingdom: economic planning regions and agricultural problem
areas referred to in the text

Anglia Economic Development Council, for instance, identified two agricultural areas – North Norfolk and the Isle of Ely – as areas of low growth. Of these, the former, though about fifty miles long, extends only a dozen miles inland from the coast and, at its nearest, is only about that distance from the considerable urban centre of Norwich. The Isle of Ely is smaller, and a good deal of it is within a dozen miles of either Cambridge or Peterborough. Both of these areas had, in 1966, over a quarter of their employment, and probably rather a higher proportion of their occupied population (including the self-employed), in agriculture. The number of agricultural employed was falling by about 3 per cent a year. There was some net outward migration of people of working age (in North Norfolk more than offset in the sixties by influx of retired people) and an increase of commuting to work out of the areas over distances of, often, something like twenty miles. Total population remained nearly steady. Male unemployment tended to be a little above the national average; female unemployment was very low.

This amounts to a combination of events that is, understandably, regretted locally, and some parts of it – the unemployment and the long-distance commuting to work – signified a waste of resources. The whole scale of the problem presented, however, was very modest. Within a region of rapid employment growth (as East Anglia as a whole was) the social and economic costs of the decline of agricultural employment in these islands of territory that it mildly dominated were not high.

Central Wales presents a rather different version of the problem. There the physical scale is greater: an area of 2,000 square miles with a population of 85,000 (about the same as in each of the two smaller East Anglian areas just discussed), with no town of more than 6,500. The proportion of the occupied population engaged in agriculture (mostly as self-employed rather than employees) must approach a third. The decline in employment in agriculture in the early sixties was just about matched by the rise in service trades, but the number in self-employment also fell; the total population showed a slow natural increase more than offset by net outward migration amounting to nearly 0·66 per cent a year. Total population fell by more than 0·33 per cent annually.

An area of this kind is too large and remote for outward commuting to work to play much part in solving its employment problem, and its towns are too small and remote from main

71

communications to present much attraction to incoming industry. The holiday trades and the provision of services for people who move in to retire, or who keep second homes in the area, provide a more promising basis for growth, though still not a very certain or large one. The acquisition of second or retirement homes, indeed, hastens the departure of the indigenous population by creating a housing shortage, or by giving them the tempting opportunity to sell and move. What is happening is a change of use of housing from the operating capital of agriculture to residence and tourist trade, and of land also to what is, in some sense, a less intensive agricultural use, combined increasingly with a recreational one. The pressure for change comes as much from the growth of the new use as from the decline of the old, and is hard to resist. Welsh nationalist opinion resents it bitterly, partly because it involves the decline of established Welsh communities, and partly because of the very general resentment of the incoming foreigner, even when he brings cash in hand. The government's remedy is to promote the growth of at least one of the small towns of the area (Newtown in the first instance) into a somewhat larger one, adequate to support a little industry. In this way, if the policy is successful, an enlarged local urban community will replace a declining local rural one, where otherwise the total and, still more, the locally rooted population would continue to decline.

By far the biggest, in extent, of the *prima facie* agricultural problem areas of Great Britain is the Highlands and Islands of Scotland, which comprises about a fifth of the area of the United Kingdom – 14,000 square miles – and contained a population in 1971 of only 283,000. This is an area with a long history of depopulation. The seven crofting counties passed their individual population maxima at various dates between 1830 and 1860: their collective maximum population (*c* 1840–50) was 400,000. It fell to 340,000 by 1911, and thereafter by 50,000 in the following twenty years, an average annual rate of 0·8 per cent. The depression of the thirties (which made the traditional destinations of Highland emigration unattractive) and the Second World War brought the rate of decline sharply down, however, to a very low level. In the fifties it rose to 0·33 per cent a year, but it fell again in the sixties almost to zero, and by the mid-seventies there was a net increase.

For the area as a whole, therefore, we seem to have only the tail-end of a depopulation problem. It is true that the area is

72

losing by net emigration nearly all its natural increase, but the same is true, virtually, of Scotland as a whole. For the area as a whole, also, we have only the tail-end of a specifically agricultural problem. Out of the total working population (of about 105,000) only about 12 per cent were, in the early sixties, engaged full time in agriculture, though another 12 or 15 per cent were partially dependent on it – most of them being crofters, smallholders with a variety of occupations, including handicrafts and miscellaneous seasonal employment. In terms of equivalent full-time occupations, agriculture probably accounted for about 20 per cent of the total active manpower, manufacturing for only about 10 per cent, and services for the remarkably high remainder, 70 per cent, a result partly of the considerable dependence on tourist trade (hotels and boarding houses accounted for about four times the UK average proportion of employment) and partly of the costliness of providing many services to the population of such a scattered community.

During the 1960s, the number engaged in agriculture seems to have fallen by about 4,000 (4 per cent of the occupied population); the growth of service employment was about equal to this, and there was a rise of some 1,500 in employment in manufacturing. Over this period, therefore, total employment rose slightly.

If one looks at the Highlands and Islands in greater detail, of course, the impression is modified. Between 1951 and 1971, the Islands (as opposed to the mainland) lost 14 per cent of their population; the mainland (containing over two-thirds of the total) made a gain of 6 per cent. The few towns are generally growing; within this large area of sparse population, net outward migration and slow growth, some geographical concentration and urbanisation of population are proceeding. The general view has been that, although something can be done to stabilise many of the small and remote communities, viable agriculture depends on consolidation of holdings, which will mean some continuation of this process. For the area as a whole, growth, because it must be largely non-agricultural, is regarded as being necessarily concentrated at a few growth points.

How far did this area constitute a problem – a challenge to policy? It did so partly because local people do not like a situation in which there is virtually no net expansion of employment opportunity in the area, the more so because the long history of absolutely declining population provides a gloomy background.

73

Partly it did so because of a sentimental regard (largely on the part of outsiders) for the values of the remaining crofting communities, which are different from those found elsewhere in Britain, and were once characteristic of the Highlands. More substantial ground for concern was the high rate of unemployment – about twice the Scottish average. A large part of it was seasonal; almost a third of the annual average amount would have disappeared if the figure could have been held at the summer minimum. Another large part was attributable to the geographical dispersion of people and job opportunities. Some must be attributed to the ease with which a certain dependence on unemployment benefits is incorporated into the crofting way of life. Most of the rest was no doubt due to the deficiency of effective demand which gives rise to the heavy outward migration. A further cause for concern is the lowness of Highland real incomes, which must also be blamed on this deficiency of labour demand, and regarded as one of the means by which it promotes emigration. But, when all is said and done, it can hardly be maintained that the area presented, even before the development of North Sea oil in the seventies, an urgent case for measures of improvement.

The development of North Sea oil in the first half of the seventies made a big difference to the Highlands and the neighbouring area of north-east Scotland centred on Aberdeen. It was estimated that, by the middle of 1975, direct additional employment in Scotland on oil installations and the like amounted to 19,000, to which should be added perhaps 10,000 extra jobs in providing the extra inputs required by the activities in question and an amount of additional Scottish employment generated by the spending of all these extra incomes which might be something like 8,000–10,000 jobs immediately, but which would probably build up in the course of time to as much as 20,000.

Of the additional direct employment, nearly a third (6,000) was in the Highlands and Islands area and more than a third (7,000) in the neighbouring parts of north-east Scotland. Both of these areas seem likely to have increased their employment on account of the oil developments, directly and indirectly, by about 10 per cent. The incidence of this was, of course, uneven. Unemployment in and near the coastal centres at which the work is mainly concentrated sank to well below the national average, whereas in one of them, the Invergordon area on the Moray Firth, it had been as high as 15 per cent in the recession of 1971. The Shetlands, where more than half the oil was planned to come ashore by pipeline, and to be transferred to tankers, negotiated a financial arrangement with the oil companies (partly in the form of compensation for disturbance) which would convert the local authority into one of the richest, in relation to population, in the country. But for most of the large area of the Highlands and Islands the development has naturally brought a much milder diffusion of prosperity from the recreational activities of immigrant executives and technicians and greater opportunity to profit by moving to the new, relatively small, boom areas of Scotland rather than to England or overseas.

NORTHERN SWEDEN

The Highland problem, such as it is, suggests comparison with those of the northern parts of Scandinavia, of which northern Sweden may stand as an example. There the area concerned is three-fifths of that of the whole country – over 100,000 square miles, with an average population density not much more than half that of the Scottish Highlands. The historical background is very different from that of Scotland; this is not an area which has long suffered from overpopulation in relation to its sparse agricultural and forest resources, but one in which colonisation, land reclamation and forest exploitation with various forms of government assistance were at their peak fairly recently and promoted increasing employment until the 1930s. A high rate of natural increase in the north, however, together with increasing relative prosperity in the south of the country, produced a northern population above equilibrium size, and thus net outward migration. Falling absolute population followed. In the early sixties the population of the north of Sweden was falling at a rate of some 0·6 per cent a year, though this rate subsequently declined sharply.

The Swedish situation illustrates in an extreme form the problems of sparsely inhabited agricultural (or forest) regions in advanced countries. Their essence is that normal community life with a high standard of living cannot be maintained unless one has centres to which quite large numbers of people have access for purposes of education, health and hospital care, shopping and entertainment. Swedish authorities put the minimum population for a fairly full range of services at about 30,000. With the kind of population density found in the north (and allowing for a fair proportion of the population living in the towns themselves but the rest widely dispersed), this means that some people will have to live thirty-five or forty miles from such centres – their access to them can hardly be described as easy, even if (at high cost) road communications are made reasonably direct and good.

At a more elementary level of provision, a community of 3,000, living in one place, is regarded as the smallest for which the usual educational and health services can be provided at reasonable cost. It has been calculated that forestry (the only obvious major occupation in much of the north) does not provide enough work within daily travelling distance of such a settlement to justify the minimum size. Forestry workers largely, therefore, live in camps from which they get home only at the weekend, if then. Without some additional basic activity (that is, an activity not directed to the servicing of the local people) forestry does not support a settled resident population. If people are to live largely away from their families, or in family dwellings remote from communities (like Australian sheep stations, for instance) then, in an advanced country where the people in question are reasonably well educated and mobile, high pay is generally necessary as an inducement – 'isolation money', one might call it. This, in turn is practicable only where the physical productivity of people in these remote situations is especially high, or where the products they provide are either unobtainable from more accessible places or protected against the competition of easier sources. Where this is not so, the thinly inhabited areas remain inhabited at all only for the (quite sufficient) reason that some people like it there. Or rather, this would be so if governments did not take the view that to leave great areas almost uninhabited is strategically undesirable. To some extent this is the view taken of northern Scandinavia, as, in very different climatic conditions, it has been the view taken of northern Australia.

This small series of examples of agricultural problem areas is characteristic of the industrial countries of north-western Europe. In Britain, as we have seen, the urgency of the problems tends to be low. The rest of Western Europe presents problems mostly of a different order of magnitude, inasmuch as the processes of industrialisation and urbanisation have gone generally less far there, and are proceeding at greater absolute rates in relation to the whole population. In the United Kingdom, at one extreme, the percentage of the population engaged in agriculture fell by less than 3 percentage points between 1950 and 1971, and in the latter year stood at just under 3 per cent; in Italy, at the other extreme, it fell by 25 points to about 19 per cent. Spain showed a reduction of 19 points in the agricultural labour force as a percentage of the total, while Ireland, Germany, Denmark, Austria, Portugal, Norway, Sweden and (perhaps) France all showed shifts of more than 10 points. In terms of this particular index of structural change, these twenty years have seen Germany accomplish what Great Britain achieved in the sixty years from the 1830s to the 1890s, Italy accomplish a good deal more, and a wide range of other European countries manage a rate of change of structure faster than the fastest rates that Britain seems ever to have shown. (She showed it over twenty-year periods in the early, and again in the late, nineteenth century.)

THE SOUTH OF ITALY

Italy presents a striking and important case not only because the change in the structure of her labour force has been so rapid, but also because the growing, industrial sector of her economy is highly localised, and because there are in any case big inter-regional differences of culture and historical background – the classic prescription for a 'regional problem'.

Southern Italy, roughly, south and east of Rome, ranks as an agricultural problem region by virtue of the fact that, in 1951, as much as 57 per cent of its total employment was in agriculture, and that its general level of income per capita was only about half that of the rest of the country; its poorest province, indeed, showed an average income only about a third of that of the country's richest. The discrepancy, moreover, had been increasing. In some ways, the Italian south may be regarded as an over-populated, poor agricultural region, similar to some others that are to be found around the Mediterranean except that it happens to be united politically with another region which has been climbing rapidly towards the general level of development of industrial Western Europe. It is handicapped by drought or unreliable rainfall and overextension of arable cultivation leading to soil erosion, and has suffered from generally inadequate size and fragmentation of holdings. Technical improvement, irrigation and reform of land tenure have achieved a good deal, but cannot by themselves overcome the basic climatic difficulties allied to an excessive agricultural population. The rate of natural increase of

77

Italy: economic planning regions

population in the south is high, much higher than in the north. Ever since the unification of Italy in the 1860s (and, indeed, before that) the south has been behind the north, though at the time of unification the difference in living standards was apparently moderate. Unification, and the very considerable development of communications within the south that followed it, seem eventually to have had a polarising effect. In the first generation, both industry and agriculture in the south grew. In the second, such industry as there was in the region declined under the pressure of northern competition. These, however, were changes of moderate strength in a period of slow national development. The rapid growth of the Italian economy came late – from the beginning of this century onwards. It took the form primarily of industrialisation, and the new manufacturing industry was situated almost entirely in the north, not surprisingly in view of that region's already established industrial lead and its greater proximity to the rest of industrial Europe.

Meanwhile, rapid population growth made land increasingly scarce in the south; a pattern of land tenure in which large landowners seem to have lacked the will to promote improvement and small peasant proprietors lacked the means (if not the will also) did not help. The result was massive emigration. In the thirty years before the First World War, there was a net outflow of more than 1 per cent of the population annually. The checking of this outflow between the two World Wars, both by American immigration restrictions and by Italian fascist policy, accentuated the pressure on the land. The excessive encouragement of wheat-growing in the interests of self-sufficiency had deleterious effects also, by tending towards soil erosion. In these ways, the south became an agricultural slum, not subsequently improved by the physical damage of the Second World War.

The main features of Italian development since the war have been a great acceleration of economic growth generally, and a conscious effort of policy to redress the relative and absolute disadvantages of the south. In some ways these two features have worked together, in some ways in opposition. Rapid economic growth has meant, throughout Italy, an accelerated development of manufacturing industry and an accelerated decline of employment in agriculture, and, other things being equal, this was bound to work to the relative disadvantage of the more heavily agricultural regions. In fact, the *proportionate* decline of agricultural employment has not been very different in the major geographic divisions of the country. But, following a tendency that is seen in other countries too, it has been rather more rapid in the more industrialised north. Expressed as proportions of the total active populations, however, those leaving the land have been about twice as numerous in the south as in the north – about 28 per cent against 14.

For these refugees from agriculture, and for the net additions to population by natural increase, the extent of non-agricultural job creation in the twenty years as a whole was, however, very different in the two regions. The north produced more than one new job for every one lost in agriculture; within it, the north-west, the main industrial area, produced two. The south, on the other hand, created in other sectors fewer jobs than it lost in agriculture, it suffered an absolute fall of some 8 per cent in employment between 1951 and 1970. It should be noted however, that a fall in employment, despite population increase, is indicated by the statistics for Italy as a whole. In part it results from the fact that many women previously recorded as 'employed' in agriculture (though not full-time agricultural workers in the usual sense) did not enter paid employment when they left the land. In part it follows from the raising of the school-leaving age. The real loss of jobs, plus the natural increase of the population of working age, went, however, over the twenty years as a whole, with a massive net migration to the north and to other countries; net migration out of the south ran at about 1 per cent of total population a year – rather more in the fifties, rather less in the sixties. In consequence, population in the south, despite its higher rate of natural increase, has grown considerably less quickly than in the rest of the country.

At first sight, then, this looks like a story of regional disaster: initial concentration on a declining means of livelihood leading to heavy outward migration and an absolute decline in employment. This, however, would be a narrow view. In the first place, one has to remember that agriculture is not like manufacturing industry. Adversity in the latter means bankruptcies and loss of jobs; in the former it is more likely to mean poorer and poorer livings for those still engaged in it. A shift of population out of agriculture is normally (and certainly in this case) a symptom of development. Those who got out probably went to much more lucrative employment, since value added per employee in non-agricultural activities was higher than that in southern agriculture by about 50 per cent in the south, and by about 100 per cent in the north. Moreover, average income per capita in the south, measured at constant prices, rose by some 67 per cent between 1951 and 1964 and a further 30 per cent between 1965 and 1971. Some of this increase could be accounted for by the change of structure – people 'moving up' from the less lucrative agriculture to more lucrative sectors – but the greater part, an improvement of 40 or 50 per cent, was accounted for by increased output per capita within sectors. In the agricultural sector itself, real output per head was more than doubled, an improvement which must have depended to an important extent upon the reduction of the population pressure there. In the other sectors (in line with widespread recent experience in the advanced countries) the increase in real per capita output was smaller.

In any case, an improvement of real income per capita by 67 per cent in thirteen years (a compound annual rate of growth of 4 per cent) is a remarkably rapid one, faster than was attained in the same period in any other of the advanced 'free market' countries except Germany and Japan, and much higher than in any but a very few (Jamaica, for instance) of the less advanced. The main fact which in some views detracts from the virtue of this achievement is that the north of Italy on a similar calculation showed a higher rate of real income growth, of just over 5 per cent a year. The inter-regional income gap apparently widened.

It has been mentioned earlier that the period since 1950 was characterised by a systematic effort of policy to help the south. This, in the briefest terms, consisted first of a determined attempt to improve southern agriculture and 'infrastructure' – transport, water supply and so on – and later, in addition, the use of both strong financial incentives and direct investment by enterprises in which the state participated to inject industry into the south. It could be objected that more massive assistance on these or other lines would have diverted to the south a greater proportion of the very rapid Italian industrialisation of this period, and would thus have both reduced the net migration to the north (and abroad) and narrowed the inter-regional income gap.

The objection is, of course, formally valid. It has been noted by an Italian writer that Italy applied to her problem region in relation to the rest of the country a measure of preference that was small in comparison with that which she had applied, by means of tariffs, to Italian industry as a whole (in relation to foreign industry) in the course of promoting her national industrialisation. The relative subsidisation of southern industry was in the range 5–10 per cent of its sales; the corresponding average protection of Italian manufacturers in the Italian market (in pre-EEC days) was 20–40 per cent. (The point is, indeed, a more general one; the highest degree of relative subsidy applied to assisted areas in the United Kingdom, similarly measured, was only perhaps 3–5 per cent, though in this case it was assisted by control of industrial building.) Regional industrial development has not been promoted by the Italian or any other government as vigorously as the same governments have sought to promote national growth at the expense of the foreigner.

It is however, hard to formulate any criterion for judging what would have been the optimum degree of diversion of industrial development to the south. The presumption is that the north has some advantages of location and also of aggregation which are lost by diverting industrial growth away from it, and there are certainly short-term costs of establishing manufacturing industry in communities that are not used to it, as opposed to bringing individuals from those communities into others with an established industrial tradition. There is no presumption that the optimum solution of the problem, economically and socially, is the one that avoids, or minimises, inter-regional migration. In the event, the surge of development in the north was far greater than the Italian authorities had dared to expect, and this greatly increased the net outward migration from the south, though at the same time it certainly relieved its agricultural poverty. Perhaps, in retrospect, it would be easier to be satisfied with the role of regional policy if it had succeeded in reducing the income gap between the regions. As things were, however, it certainly diverted to the south a greater share of the national growth than it would otherwise have had, and played some part in a regional development which, considered by itself, must be regarded as one of the most remarkable on record. Employment in industry (starting, of course, from a small base) showed a faster percentage growth than that in the rest of the country; the proportion of the occupied population that was in industry rose from a fifth to over a third, while that in agriculture fell from nearly three-fifths to about a third within twenty years.

THE WEST OF FRANCE

France's most obvious agricultural problem region is the west (Brittany, Lower Normandy and the Loire basin to which we may

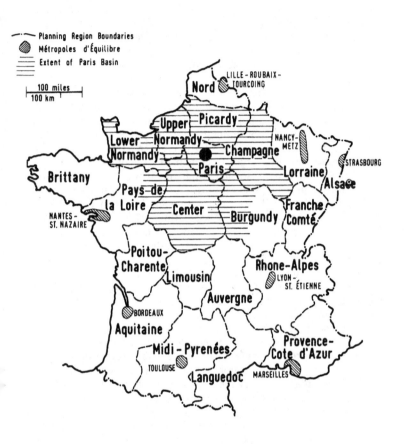

Planning Region Boundaries
Métropoles d'Équilibre
Extent of Paris Basin

100 miles
100 km

LILLE-ROUBAIX-
TOURCOING
Nord

Upper Picardy
Lower Normandy
Normandy
NANCY-
METZ
Champagne
STRASBOURG
Paris
Lorraine
Alsace

Brittany

Pays de
la Loire
Center
Burgundy
Franche
Comté

NANTES-
ST. NAZAIRE

Poitou-
Charente
Rhone-Alpes
Limousin
LYON-
ST. ÉTIENNE

BORDEAUX
Auvergne

Aquitaine

Midi-Pyrénées
Provence-
Cote d'Azur
TOULOUSE
Languedoc
MARSEILLES

France: planning regions and métropoles d'équilibre

83

add the Massif Central region comprising Auvergne and Limousin). These areas contain about a sixth of the total French population. Agricultural conditions are less adverse there than in most of southern Italy, but the proportion of the occupied population in farming is high – 48 per cent in 1954 falling to 30 per cent in 1968. Agricultural productivity is generally lower than in the rest of France. Household incomes, moreover, averaged nearly 30 per cent less than in the country as a whole, and less than half of those in the Paris region.

In the period 1954–62, the working population in agriculture was declining by about 2·5 per cent a year; over 1 per cent of the region's total working population was annually coming off the land. The increase of jobs in manufacturing, mining and construction took up only something like a tenth of this outflow; the service industries (the largest sector in this region) failed to take up more than half of it, so that employment was falling by something more than 0·3 per cent a year – though, as in southern Italy, various factors (including in this case some influx of the retired) led to a slow increase of total population. Although the natural increase of the population in some of the agricultural provinces, notably those of the south-west, was rather slow, it is not surprising that more than 0·5 per cent of the working population was being lost by net emigration annually. This may be taken as typifying the course of events in an agricultural region of an advanced European country if that region is not industrialising, but the country as a whole is.

After about 1962, the picture changed. The run-down of the numbers in agriculture continued at almost the same rate (in relation to the total population) but the rate of creation of non-agricultural jobs in the regions, particularly the west, improved to such an extent that they more than compensated for those lost in agriculture – manufacturing being responsible for most of the improvement. Net outward migration fell to less than half of what it had been. Over the period 1954–68 as a whole, these regions had lost working population by migration to a considerable extent, but the improvement in the sixties was a striking one. It is tempting to attribute it to the strengthening of regional policy – both controls on building in the Paris region and the provision of incentives to build elsewhere – which was developing strongly over the years 1958–64. The evidence is, however, not clear enough to enable this attribution to be made with great confidence. At all events, it is clear that the principal French region highly dependent upon agriculture is, like the Italian south, managing to avoid an absolute fall of population (in the sixties also absolute falls in working population) in a time of very rapid industrialisation, most of which is happening in other regions.

RURAL SPAIN

Spain, as already mentioned, had experienced a shift of her occupied population out of agriculture relatively faster than that of France, and not so very far below that of Italy. Her development, however, shows a smaller tendency towards geographical concentration than that of either of those two countries. The tensions between the different centres of population and economic development have long contributed to the political difficulties of the Spanish state, and the recent pattern of economic growth has not been such as to diminish these tensions.

There are three main areas of industrial development in Spain, widely separated: the northern coast (the Basque provinces and Asturias), Catalonia in the north-east, and western Andalusia, running down to Cadiz Bay in the south-west; add to these the Madrid area of New Castile and most of the Mediterranean coast, where there has been rapid growth of service employment, and one is left with five of the thirteen regions, Galicia, Leon, Old Castile, Estremadura and eastern Andalusia (with a reservation about its coastal strip), as the agricultural problem area. These five regions, indeed, all had more than 60 per cent of their occupied populations in agriculture in 1950, whereas the corresponding proportions in the remaining eight regions varied between 22 (in the Basque lands) and 56 (in Asturias), the national figure being 49 per cent.

In the succeeding twenty years, development of non-agricultural activity was fastest in the originally less agricultural regions; fastest of all, in relation to their total populations, in the northern belt from the Basque provinces to Catalonia, and in New Castile, but above the national average also in Asturias and along much of the eastern coast. The fall in the agricultural population has been irregular; indeed in some regions and some large parts of the period it has grown (notably in the sixties, when this was true of Leon, the Basque provinces and the east coast). There is little tendency for this fall to be correlated with local growth of non-agricultural employment; it has been fastest, proportionately to total population, in Estremadura and eastern Andalusia, where

85

Spains planning regions

alternative employment grew relatively slowly, but nearly as fast (not very surprisingly) in the east where alternative opportunities grew fairly quickly. The decline of agriculture seems to have been due locally as much to the push of poor prospects in farming as to the local attraction of good prospects outside it. In the fifties, three of the agricultural regions (Estremadura, Galicia and Leon) acquired more than enough – in Galicia many more – new jobs outside agriculture to compensate for the fall in agricultural employment, and the other two regions nearly enough. In the sixties, however, Old Castile increased its growth of non-agricultural employment and greatly slowed its agricultural decline, while Leon, as just noted, actually increased its agricultural alongside its non-agricultural jobs; but Estremadura, east Andalusia and Galicia showed an accelerated agricultural decline, and considerably less than compensating growth elsewhere. The presumption is that emigration from them grew. It is a less plain story than is that of France or Italy, but, like theirs, it is full of movement. In many provinces, net outward migration has amounted to between 1 and 2 per cent of resident population per annum.

WEST GERMANY

Germany has shed 3 million workers from the land between 1950 and 1972, but experience there has been complicated by the fact that a large number of those working on farms in 1950 were newcomers, refugees from the east. The loss of the eastern lands, however, had the effect of making West Germany a country without any very extensive regions dependent primarily upon agriculture, though there were three areas (Rheinland-Pfalz, Bavaria and Lower Saxony) where more than 30 per cent of the occupied population was in agriculture in 1950. This was not, however, so very much higher than the proportion for the whole country – just under a quarter. There was no problem of outstandingly agricultural regions comparable with those of France or Italy. Moreover, the growth of economic activity generally – mainly, of course, non-agricultural – was so very strong in Germany that it absorbed the surplus agricultural population, the natural increase, and a great many immigrant foreign workers besides.

The result was that such acute regional agricultural problems as West Germany has had, unlike those elsewhere, have remained severe only for very short times. In the early fifties the main agricultural areas were oversupplied with labour. In this period, however, they were getting rid of it very fast. Schleswig-Holstein lost by net emigration over 18 per cent of its 1950 population by 1955; Lower Saxony lost about 10 per cent. Their combined net emigration was nearly 1½ million, and Bavaria lost almost another ½ million. In spite of natural increase, Schleswig-Holstein and Lower Saxony showed net population decreases, though the latter managed to show a small increase in total employment. Where the migrants went to becomes clear when one sees that the net immigration into Hamburg, Bremen and the industrial areas of the Rhine basin is almost equal to the numbers in question.

In the sixties, the areas that had shed population in the previous decade had resumed something like the national rate of population growth. Agricultural employment continued to decrease – in the country as a whole it fell by some 22 per cent in the five years 1961–6 alone, and the proportionate rates in the more agricultural areas were not very different from this – but expansion in the non-agricultural sectors was, in general, well able to cope with the situation. In this decade, however, it is noteworthy that the relative importance of the service sector as a sector of growth, as against manufacturing, was greatly increased – a reflection of the completion of adjustment in Germany's foreign balance and of her increased affluence.

The regions that continue to be regarded as presenting problems in West Germany are nearly all dependent to a relatively large extent on agriculture. Schleswig-Holstein with a population of 2¼ million remains little industrialised and, though its agriculture is efficient, had in the mid-sixties an average per capita income some 17 per cent below the national average. In Germany as a whole, average product per worker was less than half as great in agriculture as in the rest of the economy, so that even a good agricultural area is felt to present a problem in regard to its relative standard of living. The regions which are relatively heavily dependent on less efficient forms of agriculture are, of course, at a heavier disadvantage. This is true of the hill districts of the Böhmerwald and the Eifel. In the former, per capita income has been little more than half the national average; in the latter it was about 70 per cent of it by the mid-sixties. For all regions where continued relatively heavy specialisation on agriculture is a source of low average incomes, the encouragement of industrialisation seems to be seen by the provincial and national governments as the proper remedy, and to this end special improvements of the infrastructure and some financial help to new industrial enterprises have been applied. In comparison with France or Italy, however, the West German economy, already highly industrialised before the war, with its urban and rural areas well mixed up together (like those of the United Kingdom), and with its very rapid economic growth, has experienced little of the distinctive problems of agricultural areas on a truly regional scale.

THE SOUTHERN UNITED STATES

For a final example of a problem region that is (or has been) essentially agricultural it may be interesting to look at the southern United States. These provide, indeed, a classic case, from the middle of last century when the difference between their interest, as exporters of cotton and tobacco, and that of the northern states, seeking to build up their manufacturing industries in a sheltered national market, was one of the roots of the Civil War.

The situation in the south has been complicated by many factors, the tensions between its black and white populations, and the fact that it lost, and was devastated by, the Civil War – a war which greatly stimulated industrial development in other parts of the country. In the first major stages of industrialisation in the United States, indeed, a powerful combination of forces tended to keep that development away from the south. The first real industrial advance there was the introduction of the cotton textile industry from the 1880s onwards. The initiative in this was southern, but the initial success attracted northern capital. Cheap labour and, to a minor extent, proximity to the raw material seem to have been the foundations of this success; in 1890 southern cotton textile wage rates were some 40 per cent below those in the north. Net outward migration from most of the southern states was established by that time. But, while capital and manufacturing industry increasingly flowed into the south, and population flowed out, industrialisation and the rise of incomes towards those of the rest of the country were slow. After the First World War, the fall in agricultural prices in relation to those of manufactures worked strongly against the south, where 43 per cent of total employment was still in agriculture in 1930 (in comparison with 15 per cent in the rest of the country). Agricultural wages seem to have fallen in relation to those elsewhere in the United States even while manufacturing wages were rising relatively. The rate of natural increase of population in the south rose relatively to that in the rest of the country after the First World War; by the 1940s it was about twice as high. This was no doubt a main factor in keeping relative incomes there down, despite net outward migration.

The recovery after 1933 and the Second World War brought relief through more rapid industrial development and also improved terms of trade for agriculture. The relatively high level of national prosperity since 1939, however, coupled with the great rise in agricultural productivity, have produced an acceleration of the shift out of agriculture, the process of southern industrialisation, net migration from the south, and the relative rise of southern incomes.

The active farm population of the south fell by nearly 60 per cent between 1950 and 1969. This was a somewhat greater proportionate fall than that (just under 50 per cent) shown by the rest of the country – in contrast with the general experience in Europe, where the more heavily agricultural areas have generally shown the smaller proportionate fall in agricultural employment. It was also a bigger absolute fall – nearly $2\frac{3}{4}$ million. It amounts to about a sixth of the total labour force in 1950. Numbers of people not far short of 1 per cent of the total labour force were each year ceasing to be in agriculture.

The expansion in manufacturing employment has been only something like half the loss of jobs in agriculture, and mining employment has declined. It is the enormous expansion of employment in the tertiary occupations that has taken up the slack and, indeed, the greater part of the natural increase of population as well. The latter, over the whole period since 1940, has amounted to about 1·7 per cent a year; of this rather over 0·3 per cent has been removed by net emigration, leaving a population increase of some 1·4 per cent. Against this, total employment has risen at an average rate of about 1·6 per cent, reflecting an increase in participation rates similar to that in the country as a whole. Coupled with the fact that the levels of participation and unemployment rates are not very different from those in the rest of the country, this suggests that the effects of relatively heavy reliance upon agriculture have not had unduly unfavourable effects upon total employment growth.

The emigration from the south, however, illustrates some of the complications that one often finds in what at first looks like a simple case of population moving in response to income differences. One might suppose that, in the absence of differences of unemployment and participation rates, the driving force behind net outward emigration has been difference of income levels between the south and elsewhere. This is no doubt true. Average personal income in the south was still, in 1969, nearly 20 per cent less than in the rest of the country. The statement, in relation to emigration, however, is misleading, both because the south is not homogeneous, and because emigrants from it are far from being a random sample of its population. The south as defined for statistical purposes includes, among other states, Maryland, Delaware, the District of Columbia, Florida and Texas, all of which are relatively wealthy, and not typical of the south in their migration patterns. Moreover, the net migration from the south is the result of very different patterns of movement by the white and black populations. A group of states which are for the most part the poorest – West Virginia, the Carolinas, Georgia, Kentucky, Tennessee, Alabama, Mississippi, Arkansas, Oklahoma – lose both black and white population. At the other end of the scale, Florida, Delaware and Maryland gain both. Texas and Virginia, however, gain white population and lose black, while the District of Columbia shows the opposite combination of net movements. The resultant net outflow from the south as a whole is composed of a proportionately very small gain of white population and a proportionately very large loss of black. The growth centres within the region attract population from outside it as well as inside – the outsiders mostly white. The black population, predominantly the poorest, has a strong propensity to move out altogether. Unlike the poorer sections of many other regional populations, it shows greater mobility than the better-off.

The south's success in catching up with incomes in the rest of the country is impressive; it has been a continuing trend since at least the beginning of this century. Average personal income in the south in 1900 was only about half the national average; in 1969 it was 83 per cent of it. If one takes the poorer states of the south – those that were most notably losing population by emigration – one finds that their average personal income had risen from about 67 to about 78 per cent of the national average between 1950 and 1969. Easterlin, followed by Borts and Stein, has shown that the general convergence of regional incomes within the United States, of which this was a main element, was due more to increasing similarity between them in the ratios between agricultural and non-agricultural pursuits than to changes in the

91

relative levels, between regions, of either agricultural or non-agricultural wages. In other words, it is the decrease in its excess over the national proportion of the population that is in agriculture that has done most to improve the south's relative position. (The improvement in property incomes in the south has also apparently been important.) It is true, of course, that agriculture itself has improved greatly in the south with diversification out of cotton growing, the concentration of cotton growing in the areas where mechanisation is easiest, and the reduction of overcrowding on the land, but the active farm population of the region is now only about 7 per cent of its total labour force (against about 5 in the country as a whole) so that the level of its farm incomes is a minor factor in determining the regional average. As a whole, the south has ceased to qualify as an agricultural problem region by ceasing to be, in any important sense, an agricultural region at all.

As is already the case, or is rapidly coming to be the case in all the most advanced countries, agricultural problem areas (which once were, and in countries at even a slightly earlier stage of development still are, *the* problem regions) have shrunk to relatively small enclaves hardly meriting regional status as we have understood it here.

CHAPTER 5

Coal-Mining Problem Regions

As we have already noted, mining areas are particularly liable to present problems in the course of economic change. In the first place, many of them owe their development entirely to the presence of exhaustible deposits of the mineral they mine. Not only is their activity very largely concerned with mining, but in its absence, there is no reason why they should have developed as centres of population and economic activity at all. The significance of this, however, needs to be interpreted rather carefully. If the economically recoverable reserves of the mineral run out, or if the demand for it in world markets declines, the area is obviously faced with a problem which, other things being equal, is large in proportion to the extent of its dependence on mining. But to say that without mining it would not have developed at all is not to imply that in the absence of mining in future it will entirely lose any economic function. Some mining areas have, in the past, attracted other activities, particularly manufacturing industries, and how viable these will be once mining ceases will vary from case to case. There are plenty of examples of iron- or steel-producing areas, for instance, which developed because they were rich in coal or iron ore or both, and which, having run out of their original mineral supplies, continue their metallurgical activities with the help of imported minerals. In the particular case of coal, there are areas of manufacturing industry of many kinds that owe their development, originally, to its presence, but which continue to flourish long after the coal is exhausted, or has ceased to play a major part in their economy. Any assembly of population and industry, even in the absence of the original impulse that gathered it, once gathered, is likely to persist or to grow with a degree of success that depends on its adaptability, its accessibility and its size. The further reason for the vulnerability of mining communities is that they are frequently small, some-

93

times remote and often, by virtue of their isolation and their pre-occupation with a particular way of life, also unadaptable in their skills and their entrepreneurial ideas.

The sites of much of the past small-scale mining in many parts of the world have been completely abandoned, like the lead-mining sites of the English Pennines, or the former mining 'ghost towns' of the American west. Coal, however, is outstanding in that the scale on which it has been mined, reckoned in terms of employment, has often been large, by any standard – though, of course, there has been much (now mostly vanished) small-scale mining of coal, too. Even through the direct employment, alone, to which it has given rise, and leaving out of account the cases where the presence of coal has attracted coal-mining indus-tries, it has been the major source of income, if not of whole regions (in the rather large sense in which we are using the term), at least in very large sub-regions. It is now, in many cases, a rapidly declining source.

THE WORLDWIDE COAL INDUSTRY

To anyone acquainted with the recent history of the coal industry in the United Kingdom, or in Western Europe generally, it is natural to suppose that, largely under the pressure of competition from other fuels, the industry is everywhere shrinking rapidly, both in its output and, still more, in its employment. This, how-ever, is not the case, and it is worth looking briefly at the extent and root causes of the problem coal presents to areas dependent on the demand for it, before considering how some of these areas have coped with them.

Coal is, of course, primarily a source of energy, and the world demand for energy has risen, and is rising, very fast – at some-thing like the same rate as total real income. Among the sources of energy, however, demand has been switching from coal, which was overwhelmingly the most important fifty years ago, to petroleum, natural gas and, in minor degrees, to water power and nuclear energy. The reasons are various; convenience and ease of handling liquid and gaseous fuels as compared with solid fuels is an important and longstanding one; so is the change in the technology of energy use – the growing importance of internal combustion engines in particular. Change of relative price has also played a considerable part; from the fifties to the late sixties the relative price of petroleum fell. For these and other reasons

94

petroleum and natural gas now provide some 65 per cent of the energy used in the world. In the United States coal provides only about a fifth; in the United Kingdom its share is still over a half.

A peak of British coal production was reached in 1913, and that of the United States about 1920, but in the world as a whole output has continued to grow. The rate of increase declined sharply from the beginning of the First World War, but from about 1950 it rose again. The countries in active but earlier stages of industrialisation – Japan, India, the Soviet Union, China and many others – show high rates of increase in coal production. From about 1960, output in the United States, long stagnant or in decline, began to grow again also. On a world scale, this is far from being a declining industry. Moreover, its long-term prospects on that scale are not necessarily bleak. At a time when it is widely believed that expanding demand for petroleum will begin to run seriously against shortages of total natural reserves well before the end of the present century, it may be noted that the probable reserves of coal in the world are estimated at anything up to a thousand times present annual output. Nuclear power may compete increasingly with coal for some purposes (notably generation of electricity), but where hydrocarbon fuels are needed, for the internal combustion engine or for the chemical industry, coal, by hydrogenation or otherwise, provides alternatives to petroleum and natural gas, and it will become increasingly competitive as these become scarcer and dearer. Indeed, the action of the Arab oil-exporting countries after the war of October 1973 resulted in a quadrupling of the world price of oil, which has made coal very much the cheaper source of heat-energy, though whether this relative position will persist is not clear.

What, then, is the reason for the decline of coal-mining employment that gives rise to problem areas in a number of countries? It is in the older industrial countries that this has happened, and the basic reason for it is that coal mining was developed there on a large scale in what one may call 'the Coal Age', before competing fuels began to make serious inroads; in general, before 1914. In the coal-producing countries that were at all highly industrialised by then, subsequent events have worked to produce problems in their mining areas in four ways. First, there is the competition of other fuels, to which we have referred. Second, there is increasing economy in the use of coal in, for instance, power generation and steel making – coal requirements per unit of output have fallen in these industries by about a third in the last generation. Third, labour productivity in mining has risen rapidly, more than doubling within fifteen years in the United Kingdom, for instance. Finally, the more accessible reserves in coalfields which have been mined for a long time have in some cases become exhausted and production has been concentrated on the fields that are still most profitable.

So far as the very widely differing national experiences of the coal industry are concerned, what has just been said can largely be summarised for a number of countries as shown in Table 1.

Table 1 *Annual percentage rates of change in coal output and employment in the major coal-producing countries, 1953–73*

	Output 1953–63	Employment	Output 1963–73	Employment
Belgium	– 3·2	– 6·1	– 4·7	– 4·9
United Kingdom	– 1·1	– 4·6	– 3·0	– 4·2
France	– 0·8	– 3·9	– 3·9	– 4·1
USA	– 0·4	– 8·0	2·6[1]	– 1·2[1]
Canada	– 4·4	– 7·4	7·6	n.a.
Czechoslovakia	4·1	n.a.	0·0	– 2·8
Japan	1·0	– 7·8	– 4·1[2]	– 6·8[2]
West Germany	0·7	– 6·4	– 2·8	– 4·5
USSR	2·7	n.a.	2·3	n.a.
Poland	3·2	1·0	3·3	0·0
India	6·3	2·9	1·2	n.a.
South Africa	4·1	n.a.	3·7	n.a.
Australia	3·1	n.a.	6·8	0·4[3]

[1]1960–71 (including brown coal)
[2]1963–71
[3]1960–70
Source: United Nations

The countries that already produced and used a lot of coal, even if they have continued to show rapid rates of growth of demand for energy, have seen coal production decline or grow only slowly because they were adjusting to a different (both a technologically new and a high-income) pattern of energy sources, whereas those starting more nearly from scratch have increased their demand for coal alongside that for other sources of energy. They have also been demanding energy according to a lower-income (or less consumer-oriented) pattern, in which coal occupies a larger place. And employment in coal mining has everywhere declined in relation to physical output. This is the background against which the fortunes of particular coal-mining regions within countries have to be examined.

REGIONAL DIFFERENCES IN PRODUCTION AND GROWTH

Within each of the older industrial countries, where regional problems connected with coal mining have arisen, there have been very considerable differences between coalfields. The coalfields with the highest productivity per man in their respective countries – the Campine field in Belgium, the Lorraine field in France, the Ruhr in Germany, the east Midlands in the United Kingdom, and the Illinois field in the United States – commonly show levels between 50 and 100 per cent above those with the lowest productivities. It is not easy to generalise as to whether these productivity levels have been converging or diverging in the fifties and sixties. In France and Belgium there has been a divergence; the better fields have shown more improvement than the worse ones. In Germany, Lower Saxony has tended to catch up with the Ruhr, but the Saar and Aachen fields have been falling farther behind. In the United Kingdom, the leading east Midlands field has shown the lowest improvement of all, with Yorkshire (the second best) catching up; among the fields with lower levels of productivity, Scotland and Durham have gained on the national average, the north has roughly kept up with it, while the north-west and south Wales (the latter very much the lowest in productivity) have fallen farther behind. The United States shows a not dissimilar pattern, with the leader, Illinois, tending to lose its lead to Kentucky, but with the lowest-productivity field, Pennsylvania, falling farther back.

Insofar as labour productivity is an indicator of general economic efficiency (as it tends to be in an industry as labour-intensive as coal mining), one might expect the fields with the highest absolute productivity to show the greatest growth, or the smallest decline, in production. This proves to be very broadly true within most of the countries we are examining. In Belgium, the Sud field's share of total national output suffered a sharp fall from 66 to 40 per cent between 1955 and 1968 – its absolute output fell by almost three-quarters. In France the Nord and Centre-Midi fields lost some 40 per cent of their former output, while

97

Lorraine's was almost maintained. In the United Kingdom, the Yorkshire and east Midland fields increased their share of national output from 43 to 55 per cent; they suffered less than 10 per cent falls in absolute output, while other fields lost 40 or 50 per cent; though the field that showed the biggest fall in production was not south Wales (with the lowest productivity) but the north-west. In the United States, the relatively small but high-productivity Illinois and Kentucky fields increased both their absolute output (by about 40 per cent) and their share of national output. The Pennsylvania field was the only one to suffer an absolute fall in production; the large West Virginia field slightly increased its output but fell back in its percentage share of the national total. In West Germany, where the Ruhr dominates, with over four-fifths of total output, that great field's production fell by a quarter, as did the national total. Of the smaller fields, all with lower labour productivities, Lower Saxony and Aachen, however, gained relatively (the latter absolutely), but the Saar suffered almost a 40 per cent fall in output level.

Factors other than the average level of labour productivity evidently play some part in determining the relative fortunes of coalfields within a national market, and some of these factors are fairly plain. One is that conditions within a field may be far from uniform; it is possible for new coalfaces to be in process of being opened up by modern, high-productivity methods while coal is still being acquired under more adverse conditions nearby. The marginal cost may be very different from the average cost in the field, and the relation between the two may differ widely from one field to another. (Indeed, if two fields with similar marginal costs have marginal cost curves rising at different rates, the one with the steeper curve will presumably tend to show the lower average cost, and the smaller response of output to a fall in demand – but also the smaller response to a rise.)

Secondly, geographical position in relation to the consumers, and the economic fortunes of the field's main consumers, both play a part. On the large geographical scale this is certainly important. Most of the enormous coal resources of the United States outside the most heavily worked fields have hardly been exploited at all. On the smaller scale of Western Europe, where the coalfields are not very far from major centres of population and industry, it is less significant. It is true that, in the United Kingdom, for instance, there is some correlation between the changes in production of coal in the various regions and the changes in its consumption in them – both have fallen most (proportionately) in the north-west, while in Yorkshire and the midlands, where, as we have noted, production was well maintained, consumption was well maintained also. But it must be remembered that the most buoyant part of consumption – that of the electricity-generating industry – tends to be located where the cheapest coal is, and to export its power to other regions. Finally, it has to be remembered that coal is not a homogeneous product, and the particular demands for the coals from different fields have fared differently.

For whatever reasons, however, it is clear that some coalfields have suffered particularly sharp contractions in output, and, because of the general rapid increase in labour productivity, the fall in mining employment, which extends to every major coalfield in Western Europe and the United States, has in some cases been very severe indeed. Between 1955 and 1968, more than half the mining jobs disappeared in the Pennsylvania field, in the Scottish, Welsh and northern English fields, (though not Yorkshire or the midlands), in all the German fields except the small one around Aachen, in the Sud field in Belgium, (where the loss was over three-quarters) and in the central and southern French fields. In these years the loss of mining jobs amounted to nearly 90,000 in south Belgium, nearly 57,000 in the northern French field, some 60,000 each in south Wales and Durham, and over a quarter of a million in the Ruhr. The total loss in all the countries mentioned was of the order of a million.

DEPENDENCE ON COAL

One would expect the problem with which coal-mining areas are faced when their main industry declines to be severe in proportion to the rate of disappearance of coal-mining jobs as a proportion of their total employment or, perhaps better, of their total male employment. This in turn obviously depends on the local rate of shrinkage of the industry and the area's degree of dependence upon it. The former of these elements we have already looked at; the degree of dependence also requires some attention.

It is a rather more elusive concept, because the proportion of the population engaged in a particular industry is so sensitive to variation in the boundaries of the area at which one looks. If one considers a relatively small area, or a collection of selected small areas, such as the 'coal counties' of Virginia or Kentucky, or at west Durham or south Wales, one can find instances (including

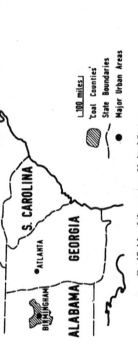

Coalfields of the eastern United States

Northumberland and Durham coalfields

those just mentioned) where coal mining provided, a generation ago, half or more of all male employment. Since it is (or has been) characteristic of coalfields that there is relatively little female employment, this implies that the proportion of total employment provided by coal mining has also been high in these areas – often more than a third. If however, one looks at rather wider areas that function as 'regions' in the sense that they possess a fair degree of self-sufficiency where most of the service industries are concerned, the proportion of even male employment provided by coal mining is naturally smaller; in Wales, the northern region of England, the Nord region of France, and the state of West Virginia, for instance, it varied, twenty years ago, between 15 and 25 per cent.

Data are not available for the different coalfields that are comparable with each other in all respects, particularly in the periods to which they relate. One can say, however, that in the mining areas (fairly narrowly defined) where contraction of mining employment can be called severe, this employment has been falling at a rate of more than 1 per cent of *total* male employment in the area per year, sometimes much more. Thus in the Pas-de-Calais département (total population 1·4 million) and in west Durham, the rate has been 3 to 3·5 per cent. In the Hainaut province of Belgium (total population 1·3 million) and in the 'coal counties' of West Virginia it has been nearly 2 per cent. In the Ruhr coalfield, with a total population of about 5 million, it was about 1·2 per cent. But in wider, 'regional' areas, the Nord region of France, the four British regions most heavily engaged in coal mining, the states of Kentucky and Pennsylvania, and the Land Nordrhein-Westfalen, the corresponding rate varied around 0·5 per cent of total male employment a year. In the state of West Virginia (population 1·75 million) however, it must have been over 1 per cent.

How did the coalfields, and the wider areas of which they formed part, cope with these changes? First, what was the effect on total male employment? West Durham provides one of the most severe cases; there the coal-mining employment fell by some 38,000 or 40 per cent of the initial male labour force between 1951 and 1970 (mostly in the second half of that period). The *total* male employment contracted by about half this amount – nearly 20 per cent of its 1951 figure. In the sixties, those parts of west Durham where the degree of dependence on mining was above the average suffered a fall of almost 30 per cent in total

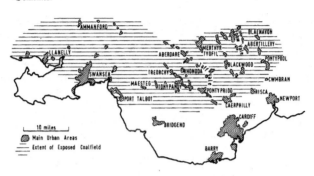

South Wales coalfield

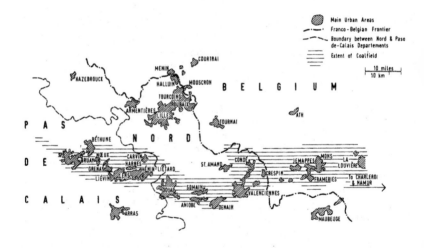

The Franco–Belgian frontier area

male employment. In the wider region within which all this happened, the northern region, total male employment fell in the sixties by some 6 per cent.

South Wales is another severe case, though with marked local variations. Some tendency is visible there for the percentage fall in coal employment to be highest where the degree of dependence on it was greatest. In those districts where more than half the employment was in coal mining in 1961, about 58 per cent of the total coal employment of the sub-region was situated, but these areas bore 66 per cent of the reduction in the succeeding nine years. In them, the decline of mining employment amounted to something like 30 per cent of initial total employment; their total employment fell by 22 per cent. At the other end of the scale, however, in the areas least dependent upon coal, the fall in total employment was rather greater than that in mining employment. In the sub-region as a whole, it was about a third as great: 12 per cent of the 1961 male employment, as against 35 per cent.

In France, experience in the Pas-de-Calais was broadly similar; the loss of 65,000 jobs in coal mining resulted in a reduction of about half that amount in total male employment. In the Nord region as a whole, one has to take account of the fact that mining was not the only – or the most important – declining industry. Numbers occupied in agriculture fell by 41,000 (3 per cent of total active population) between 1954 and 1962; numbers in mining fell by 29,000 and those in textiles by the same number, while the total occupied population fell by 28,000.

The Ruhr coalfield lost some 200,000 coal-mining jobs in the 1960s, virtually halving its employment in this industry; the loss amounted to probably something like 7 per cent of the total occupied population. What happened to total employment and to the total occupied population in this precise area is somewhat obscure; it is significant, however, that total resident population remained virtually stationary, whereas in the remaining two-thirds (by population) of the Land Nordrhein-Westfalen it rose by about 11 per cent. Of the administrative districts (Regierungs-bezirke) into which the Land Nordrhein-Westfalen is divided, total male employment fell in the three where parts lie on the coalfield (Düsseldorf, Münster and Arnsberg) between 1961 and 1970, and rose in the other three. The fall of the total male employment varied, however, as a proportion of the fall in mining employment; it was almost equal to it in Arnsberg and Düssel-dorf, but only a third as big in Münster, notwithstanding that the

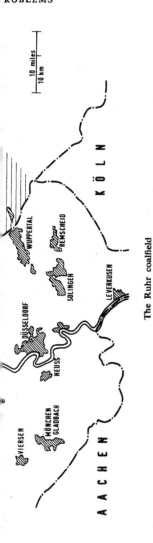

The Ruhr coalfield

degree of dependence on coal was initially greatest in the last-mentioned area.

In the United States, the biggest reduction in mining employment came in the 1950s. Those counties that, at the beginning of that decade, had more than 40 per cent of their total labour force (perhaps 55 per cent of their male labour force) in mining lost coal-mining jobs in the decade amounting to 29 per cent their total (male and female) employment in 1950. Here, again, there was another declining industry, namely, agriculture, but in this case its contribution to employment decline was much smaller than that due to coal mining. Industries outside mining and agriculture achieved only a small offsetting increase, and total employment fell by nearly a third. Those counties in which mining provided least (on average 4·2 per cent) of the total employment in 1950, on the other hand, lost mining jobs constituting only 2·6 per cent of their total 1950 employment, and managed a growth of 4 per cent in employment in the decade, despite some loss of jobs in agriculture also. Employment outside mining and agriculture showed a *percentage* rate of growth that was, broadly, highest where the impact of the mining run-down on total employment was least, thus suggesting that the multiplier effect of falling mining (and agricultural) employment on either technically linked or local service industries was somewhat greater than what might be called the 'replacement effect' – the attraction of new industry by the supply of labour released from the declining activities.

ADJUSTMENTS TO CHANGE

As coal-mining employment fell in the areas in question, what happened to their populations? As with the agricultural populations we have considered, or any others whose previous means of livelihood disappear, there are the possibilities of finding other work in the same area, of continuing to live there while commuting to work in some other area not too far away, of moving out in search of work, or of retiring from the labour force sooner than they otherwise would. In the shorter run, a failure to adopt any of these solutions will add the people concerned to the numbers of the unemployed. One must qualify these remarks, however, by noting that it is not absolute fall in employment as such that presents these alternatives; it is failure of changes in the number of jobs to match the independent changes in the number of people who are of working age and who wish to be employed. If the course of birth and death rates has been such that the population of working age in a region is falling, a corresponding fall in the number of local job opportunities obviously does not present the kind of problem with which we are concerned. If the population of working age is increasing, on the other hand, through excess of numbers arriving at working age over deaths and retirements, then even a rising number of job opportunities may be inadequate to prevent a regional problem from arising.

The British coalfields for a long time showed rates of natural increase well above the average for the country, but in varying degrees their more recent history has altered this. Coal has been a shrinking industry for over half a century, and from most of the coalfields there is thus quite a long record of net outward migration, though to widely varying extents. Migrants are normally, for the most part, young adults, sometimes with children. Outward migration therefore means that the young population of the area, and its birth rate, are reduced. Lack of inward migration means that these effects are not countered. Just as birth rate is depressed by the shift of the population structure towards the older age-groups, so the death rate, and the rate of retirement, are raised. The rate of natural increase of both the total and the working population falls.

In the two major British coalfields that have suffered heavy net outward migration over a long period, west Durham and south Wales, the rate of natural increase of population is low, whereas in, for instance, the Yorkshire and Nottingham–Derbyshire fields, which have suffered less in this way, it is still high. Their demographic history thus makes the problem of redundant labour less severe in west Durham and south Wales than it would otherwise be, but because job opportunities in coal have been shrinking there so fast, it is nevertheless a severe one. Consequently, net outward migration continues. West Durham fell in population by some 3·4 per cent between 1951 and 1966. This is much less than the fall in male employment in the same period. In south Wales again (the sub-region 'Central and Eastern Valleys') where male employment fell by 12 per cent in the sixties, total resident population also fell – but by only 0·33 per cent. To some extent the discrepancy is accounted for by the male bias of outward migration; to some extent by increased commuting to work in adjacent areas (in both cases mostly the parts nearer to the coast), to some extent by increased unemployment and early retirement from the labour force. But from smaller areas within the sub-regions, the outward shift of population was naturally more severe; the towns of Crook, Tow Law, Stanley and Bishop Auckland in west Durham all fell in population by between 8 and 15 per cent between 1951 and 1966; in south Wales, Rhondda, Abertillery and Blaenavon all fell in population by at least 14 per cent in the same period. A good deal of these heavy losses was probably due to relocation within the sub-region, but some of it certainly to higher than average propensities to move out altogether.

The historically high birth rate of the Nord region of France, still about 15 per cent above the national average in the 1960s, was responsible for returning one of the country's higher growth rates in the past twenty years. Population there grew by 16·1 per cent between 1951 and 1969. In 1962–8 it grew by 4·2 per cent, but the coal basin managed only 1·8 per cent in this period: a natural increase of 5·5 per cent was offset by a 3·7 per cent loss by net emigration. The coal towns of the Nord generally returned some of the lowest urban growth rates in the 1960s. The two main coal provinces in south Belgium (Hainaut and Liège) on the other hand, like west Durham and south Wales, show rates of natural increase well below average and, since the war, with a negative migration balance have produced little or no population growth. The outcome has been to give Liège a population growth rate (1950–69) that was only 38 per cent of the national rate and Hainaut one that was only 66 per cent of it.

In West Germany, the run-down of coal-mining employment was, of course, superimposed on very rapid economic expansion; it also followed a period in which the population of the chief mining areas, the Ruhr, had been the centre of very rapid population growth, up to 2 per cent a year, through the influx of refugees from the east. In the sixties, this rate of growth, in the three Regierungsbezirke of which parts lie on the coalfield, fell to a modest 0·5 per cent a year, though that in the Cologne district to the south remained high. There was net emigration from much of the coalfield in the later sixties, amounting to 1 to 1·5 per cent a year from some local government areas; but, to judge by the statistics of aggregate income changes, gains and losses were well mixed up together. The *Kreise* of Moers and Dortmund, for instance, did badly, those of Essen and Düsseldorf did well. It seems that there was much local movement within the Ruhr conglomeration, where chemical and metal-working activities were growing, and probably a good deal of outward movement to destinations no more than a few miles farther up the Rhine. By 1969, the coalfield as a whole had a slight inward balance of migration, almost certainly due to net inflow of foreign workers more than offsetting net outflow to the rest of Germany. The three Regierungsbezirke lying partly on the coalfield showed net migration losses to the rest of Germany; the other three net gains.

In the coal counties of Appalachia, however, much bigger population changes have taken place in a relatively short interval. Contrary to national trends, the state of West Virginia as a whole lost population in both of the two postwar decades; the other coal states of Appalachia either declined in one of these two decades or grew less rapidly than the country as a whole. As between counties, in the 1960s, initial dependence on coal and population change were very strongly related. Counties with more than 20 per cent of the total labour force dependent on coal in 1960 exhibited rates of decline often several times greater than those with a lesser dependence on it (see Table 2).

Table 2 *Total population change, 1960/70 (%)*

Coal counties of	More than 20% dependent on coal	Less than 20%
W. Virginia	− 17·9	− 5·3
Alabama		− 2·6
Kentucky	− 16·7	− 7·6
Virginia	− 13·5	− 21·3 (one county only)
Pennsylvania	− 5·7	− 0·6

Changes in the 1950s had been even more spectacular. Many coal counties had suffered losses of up to 20 to 30 per cent, with the result that in twenty years cumulative losses of up to 45 per cent of the 1950 population were recorded. Thus the presence of coal, and its decline, has almost without exception led to a contraction of population on coalfields.

Losses of this order were, of course, mainly the result of very heavy net emigration. In the coal counties of the Appalachian region the decade of most rapid change, the 1950s, saw migration balances of up to 60 per cent in this ten years – a compound average loss of 4·8 per cent a year. Not surprisingly, outward migration rates are seen to be correlated with 1950 levels of dependence on coal.

It is apparent from this that the rates of net outward migration from the Appalachian coal counties were far greater than corresponding ones out of mining areas in Europe. The geographical mobility of people generally is higher in the United States than in (at least) the United Kingdom. The representative British resident changes his house every nine or ten years, the representative American about twice as often. The British probability of changing one's standard region in any given year is about 1·5 per cent; the representative American's probability of changing his state (which is likely to mean moving a longer distance) is about 3·5 per cent. Moreover many of the mining communities of Appalachia are more remote from major centres of population than European mining communities, which diminishes the possibility of both outward commuting and tempting new industry in. The relatively small and isolated nature of many of the mining settlements, in hill country, tends to make them unsuited to other kinds of economic activity.

In some cases travelling daily to work in another area is an alternative to moving away from the coalfield altogether. In south Wales and west Durham the commuter came into his own after 1951, travelling in both cases to the neighbouring coastal areas. In west Durham between 1951 and 1966 the daily exodus of men to the east had increased by 66 per cent or 14,000, while local journeys within the coalfields increased by 20 per cent. The eight largest towns took a large share of the additional outward movement. The importance of this movement can be judged by comparing the 14,000 increase in outward commuting with the fall of 21,000 in the number of male jobs on the coalfield in the same period. A similar change is observed in South Wales where commuting to the coastal areas increased by 32 per cent so that by 1966 commuting from the coalfield to the coast represented over 50 per cent of male journeys to work involving movement to local authority areas other than the area of residence. These figures reveal nothing of the industrial or occupational nature of commuters, but the presumption is that ex-miners, or men who would otherwise have been miners, formed a large part of them.

UNEMPLOYMENT

So much, then for the movement of population out of the coal areas, either once for all or by daily commuting to work elsewhere. How far did the run-down result in those who remained being involuntarily without employment? The answer is very different for different regions and times. In the United Kingdom, for instance, the run-down of the earlier 1930s (a 28 per cent fall in employment between 1929 and 1936) went with very high unemployment of coal miners, even in relation to the level in all industries. In northern England, Wales and Scotland, the percentage of insured persons unemployed in June 1936 was 34·3 among coal miners, 18·7 in all industries together. On the other hand, up to 1967, the postwar run-down left the registered unemployment rate among coal miners below that for the whole industrial population. Changes in definition may have had something to do with this, but probably more is due to the high rate of normal retirement on account of age – the rate of recruitment of young men to the industry having long been low – and the transfer schemes of the National Coal Board. These in the sixties, moved some 11,000 miners between divisions (mostly to the longer-life coalfields of Yorkshire and the east Midlands), and perhaps eight or ten times as many between collieries within divisions. After 1967, with a more rapid rate of run-down (and probably a reduced rate of voluntary movement to other industries in the slacker labour market conditions that had arisen) the scope for shifting miners from places where they were redundant to others where they were still needed was reduced, and mining unemployment rose. It reached 7·5 per cent, an absolute figure of over 30,000, in 1971/2, but in subsequent recovery (and slow-down in mine closures) it halved.

The increase was reflected in local general unemployment rates in the affected areas. In south Wales in the period of rapid decline unemployment rates of 7 to 10 per cent occurred in many areas, including Risca, Treorchy, Tonypandy, Maesteg, Ammanford and Caerphilly, and Blackwood. Redeployment and outward migration seem to have had a more limited impact on reducing the numbers of redundant miners in this period.

West Durham's unemployment experiences were broadly similar to those of south Wales, the male unemployment rate rising from about 3 per cent in 1961 to 8 per cent in early 1963 and after that staying generally in excess of 6 per cent. Remoteness from industrial centres, the reliance on a single industry, and location within a larger region which has had more than its share of other structural adjustments all combined to produce very considerable human problems in the sub-region.

Besides registered unemployment, however, the run-down of

110

demand for coal miners has certainly led to a good deal of earlier retirement from the labour force than the men concerned would otherwise have chosen. How much this amounts to is difficult to say. After correcting for the age composition of the population, one finds the proportion of men who are retired rather higher in the main coal-mining regions than elsewhere. Regionally, the discrepancy amounts to less than 1 per cent of the labour force, but locally it is presumably more noticeable.

In the mining areas of northern France, the crude male activity rates (ratios of economically active to total male population) were in 1962 only 80·5 per cent of the corresponding rates for the Nord region as a whole, but unemployment in the Pas-de-Calais, as in the region as a whole, has been remarkably low – in the late sixties lower than in Paris. In the Mons and Charleroi arrondissements of Belgium the corresponding rates fell by 26 and 15 per cent respectively between 1947 and 1961. In the latter year, while the proportions of younger men at work seem to have been above the national average in these Belgium mining districts, the proportion of older men active was anything from 10 to 40 per cent below it. There is strong *prima facie* evidence here that early retirement from the labour force accounted for a substantial proportion of the reduction in male employment that went with the coal-mining run-down.

The Belgian adjustment was, however, assisted by a number of circumstances. First, the coal run-down occurred sharply but at a time of relatively high employment. Moreover, since more than half the mineworkers in the south were foreigners, much of the unemployment impact fell upon them, and many of them left the country. Third, the favourable location of Belgium and its small size made it far easier to place redundant men than was the case say, in the large remote areas of Appalachia or perhaps even in west Durham. The main coal provinces of the Belgium Sud coalfield (Hainaut and Liège) did however increase their share of total unemployment from 21·5 to 40·7 per cent between 1960 and 1969. There appears to be no correlation between the rate of labour release in mining and the level of unemployment except in the period of most rapid run-down, 1958–61. The rising levels of unemployment from the mid 1960s seem to be the result more of the changing location of new jobs, away from the Walloon French-speaking region of the south and towards the north and north-western areas of the country, rather than of what was happening to the coal industry itself.

111

Unemployment in West Germany was at a very low level generally in the sixties, apart from the recession of 1967–8. The remarkable fact is that, in the Regierungsbezirke that contain parts of the Ruhr coalfield, male unemployment rates remained fairly consistently below even the low national, or even the Nordrhein-Westfalen, average. This, however, did not prevent locally high rates, as in the urban areas of Gelsenkirchen and Gladbeck.

In the American mining areas, as one would expect from the rapidity of the run-down and the relative isolation of some mining communities, unemployment was locally severe. In the Pennsylvania anthracite region, an analysis of fifty-five towns showed that in 1950 thirty-five had male unemployment rates of up to 10 per cent, eighteen of 10–14 per cent, and two of between 15 and 18 per cent. By 1960 the number of towns had shifted, respectively, to ten, seventeen and twenty-eight, whereas the average male unemployment rate for the state in both years was 6 per cent. In neighbouring West Virginia, where state unemployment averaged 8·3 per cent in 1960, rates in coal counties were in some cases more than double this figure, running up to 26 per cent. Although some 88,000 miners retired under pension provisions whilst others obtained jobs in neighbouring counties, many were unable to find security of employment so that unemployment remained high for a long time. Even though the most rapid reduction of mining employment occurred in the early 1950s the unemployment rate of Appalachian coal miners was in 1957 still 6·4 per cent compared with 3·8 per cent for all industries.

FEMALE EMPLOYMENT AND MALE ACTIVITY RATES

Since coal mining is a male occupation and since coalfields have historically attracted heavy industry (or no manufacturing industry at all) job opportunities for women have been slow to develop in these areas. In some cases women have tended to move out of them to jobs elsewhere, either as daily commuters or as residents, but to a large extent they have simply adopted an outlook and way of life in which paid employment played no part. It is probable, indeed, that this has reinforced the scarcity of job opportunities for women by deterring female-employing firms from entering the areas. In recent years all this has been changing as, in many countries, the demand for female labour has grown faster than that for male – office work and light manufacturing industries that employ women as manual workers have tended to grow in relation to the rest of the economy in advanced countries. The run-down of the coal industry and the difficulties of redeployment have, moreover, tended to reduce family earnings on the coalfields, and this has probably broken down still further the tradition that women do not go out to work. At all events, the growth of female employment has in some cases played a major part in enabling the coal-mining areas to weather their difficulties.

From the available data it seems that in all the coalfields studied the picture is one of faster than average growth in female employment, partially offsetting the contractions of male employment which we have noted. The occupied female population grew by 36 per cent in South Wales, 45·5 per cent in west Durham and 11·7 per cent in the Pas-de-Calais. The contractions in male employment in combination with the growth in female have, of course, produced larger female shares of total employment, and the increase has in some cases been striking (see Table 3).

Table 3   *Female shares of employment in Britain and France*

	Female share of total employment (%)			Growth of female employment (%)	Growth of male employment (%)	Growth in total employment (%)
A.	*1951*	*1961*	*1969*	*1951–69*	*1951–69*	*1951–69*
S. Wales						
coalfield	20·4	24·1	29·4	36	− 16·8	− 6·1
Wales (Total)	26·5	29·6	33·4	36	− 5·2	4·8
W. Durham						
coalfield	20·7	24·1	32·0	45	− 19·6	− 5·8
N. Region	28·3	31·4	35·6	32	− 4·7	5·6
Gt. Britain						
(Total)	34·3	35·7	37·4	22	6·1	11·4
B.	*1954*	*1962*	*1968*	*1954–68*	*1954–68*	*1954–68*
Pas-de-Calais	24·9	26·8	28·8	11·7	− 9·0	− 4·0
Nord region	29·6	30·6	31·5	6·6	− 2·7	0·0
France (Total)	34·6	34·6	34·9	7·6	+ 6·3	+ 6·8
(Belgian data not available)						

In all these British and French cases, the coalfields' ratio of female to total employment has moved up much nearer to the national average, though in all of them it was, at the end of the sixties, still considerably below it. But the main point is that the expansion of female employment has made a substantial contribution to maintenance of employment and personal incomes in the coalfields. In the wider regions in which the coalfields lie – the north region of England, Wales and the Nord region of France – it has helped substantially to prevent a fall in total employment and in the first two cases has contributed to a small increase.

In the Pennsylvania anthracite region, also, between 1950 and 1960 female employment rose while male employment fell, but in this case the increase (6 per cent) was no greater than that in female employment in the rest of the state, and it was, in absolute numbers, less than a seventh of the amount by which male employment fell. Probably the pressure of female-employing industries to seek out reserves of female labour was less in the United States in the fifties than it was in Western Europe, though female employment was increasing much faster than male there, as it was across the Atlantic.

In general, then, experience of declining coal-mining areas supports some natural presumptions; notably that the problem is more severe, and brings heavier unemployment, the more remote the mining areas in question from other kinds of employment, as well as being dependent on the pressure of demand in the country as a whole. Germany, with her main mining area part of her biggest industrial aggregation, and with almost continuous expansion of labour demand, scored on both these points; France and Belgium did not do badly; the United Kingdom did fairly well from the start of the postwar run-down until the mid-sixties, despite the moderate remoteness of some mining areas from centres of growth (but had done very badly in the thirties); the United States in the fifties incurred all the problems of remoteness allied with not very exuberant demand, which produced both unemployment and outward migration on much larger scales than elsewhere. Some other presumptions are not so generally supported, at any rate by the data we have available. The relation between increase of unemployment and withdrawal from the labour force varies very widely between cases – the low level of French unemployment, and the sensitivity of the activity rate to labour demand is the most striking apparent anomaly in this respect. The extent to which adversity in the normally very heavily male-employing coalfields is met by increased female

114

employment is also very variable; perhaps this can be satisfactorily explained in most cases by differences in pressure of labour demand generally, but comparable data are rather hard to come by.

THE LEGACY OF COAL MINING

As we noted at the beginning of this chapter, one of the difficulties faced by some coal mining areas as the demand for labour in their main industry declines is that they are a long way from alternative existing sources of employment, and also too far off the beaten track to be attractive to incoming industry. This is least true of the big coalfields that have attracted secondary industry in their heyday: the Ruhr, the Yorkshire and Lancashire coalfields, the Nord coalfield in France and the Pennsylvania fields; though it can be very true of their outlying fringes, farthest from large centres of population.

But coalfields produce characteristics, apart from their location, which are inimical to the attraction, or generation, of alternative activities. The first is subsidence, which, apart from ruining the natural drainage of flat country, can render large areas unsuitable as sites for heavy buildings, and thus for many kinds of industry. The second is the visual ruin of the landscape, not only by derelict headgear and buildings when mines are abandoned but, more seriously, by spoil-heaps, some of them very large. The total area of derelict land in Great Britain, for instance, (much of it due to coal mining) at the end of the 1960s was estimated at 130,000 acres, and the cost of treating it (which does not necessarily mean restoring it to its original state) was estimated at more than £1,300 an acre, at 1968 prices. A particularly intractable form of dereliction, especially in some of the Appalachian coalfields, is that left by opencast or strip mining, in which the topsoil is not restored. Recent United States legislation requires restoration, and the practice in this respect has been improving, but, in all, something approaching a million acres of untreated strip-mined land exists in the United States. Both this denudation and disturbance of large areas of land and the dumping of colliery spoil on the surface may lead to the pollution of rivers by acid run-off from the areas in question.

To add to these impacts of mining on the land there is the peculiar form and quality of housing and other social capital that it leaves. Even where mining communities are not remote from centres of actual or potential alternative employment, they are not usually in the physical shape most suitable for housing employees attached to those alternative activities. Coal mining produces villages associated with individual pits and scattered over the landscape, rather like agricultural villages (though usually larger), and this state of affairs makes for long journeys to work when mining is exchanged for other employments; also for long journeys to shopping centres and to schools and colleges and for uneconomic operation (or, in consequence, absence) of public transport. The quality of much housing in mining districts is, moreover, poor; in this, however, they resemble many other old industrial districts, in which housing was erected, say, sixty to a hundred years ago, in a hurry, for tenants of modest means and to the standards of that earlier age.

All these factors handicap mining areas in the competition for incoming industrial or commercial jobs in an age when many such jobs are 'footloose' and can be placed on green-field sites in pleasant country or in established but growing communities where the social capital is on average relatively modern.

POLICY AND OUTCOMES

The governments of all the countries from which we have drawn examples took steps to assist their main mining areas. The broad regional policies of the countries dealt with are discussed in the final chapter of this book, but the peculiar circumstances and problems of coal mining have led to some measures of a specific nature, some of them emanating from the industry itself. The labour-transfer schemes of the National Coal Board in the United Kingdom have already been referred to. They were effective in preventing unemployment so long as the rate of run-down of the total labour force was moderate in relation to rates of retirement, but could not wholly cope with the more rapid contraction of the later sixties. In the old EEC countries, the European Coal and Steel Community has done much to modify and smooth the course of change. On the one hand, high-cost mines within the Community (notably the Belgium, Italian and French) were subsidised by production taxes levied on low-cost mines (mostly the German and Dutch) thus tending to equalise the rate of run-down between countries. On the other hand, from 1954 onwards, the High Authority of the Community has given assistance to former miners for readaptation to other work; this help extended, between 1954 and 1971, to some 350,000 ex-miners, as the number of mining jobs fell by about 650,000.

Specific measures for the treatment of derelict land have also, as is implied in what was said earlier, a particular relevance to mining areas. In the United Kingdom, central government grants for this purpose have long been available to local authorities, and the rate of grant has been higher in the areas given assistance under regional policy measures than elsewhere. The attack on dereliction by these means was accelerated at the end of the sixties and, as mentioned above, there has been an improvement in practice and in legal requirements concerning restoration in the United States also. There has, moreover, been more specific state aid, such as the extra assistance given to the 'Special Development Areas' in the UK from 1967.

The effectiveness of the specific policies in question can hardly be assessed in the presence of so many variations between cases, both in the general atmosphere created by national regional policies and in other factors. The presumptions seem to hold that heavy initial dependence on mining as a source of employment within what may be regarded as a practicable daily travel distance is a major creator of hazard. Remote, specialised mining districts suffer most. But the mobility of population modifies the outcome. Many mining communities in the Appalachians probably shrank more than they would have done, even given their degree of remoteness, in a country where the propensity to move was smaller. Even so, unemployment was heavy. The degree of expansiveness in the economy generally matters a great deal – the reabsorption of most of the labour force released by the German coal industry in the sixties was remarkably rapid, even given the proximity of the main German coalfields to booming centres of other activities. The nature of neighbouring activities is also important – the Pas-de-Calais coalfield suffered from having a textile district as its neighbour, though the expansiveness of the French economy enabled a growth mainly of service employment to provide an impressive degree of compensation. In comparison, in the more sluggish British economy, west Durham and the south Wales valleys have fared less well; adjustment there has been to a considerable extent by short-distance movement, or extended daily travel, within the region of which they form part, and the record of those regions, taken as a whole, has been one of only very slow growth.

Considering the extent of the run-down of coal-mining employment in the advanced economies in the last twenty years, how-ever, and the difficulties inherent in the industry's location and nature, the result can perhaps be seen best as emphasising the powers of adaptation in an economy when the general level of growth in world demand is high.

CHAPTER 6

Depressed Manufacturing Regions

The agricultural and mining problem regions which have so far been discussed in some detail raise problems mainly because they are dependent to a large extent on one industry, which, in their case at least, is not doing well. That they have reached their present levels of population and economic development may be ascribed to their having, or having once had, comparative advantages for this industry. As we have already noted, it is an important feature of their difficulties that in varying degrees the geographical pattern of habitation in them, the nature of their infrastructure (or lack of it), the skills, attitudes and ways of life of their people, and their location in relation to the great concentrations of people and industry that provide the main markets for goods and services in general, are specific to what they have been living by, and render them not very easily adaptable to other kinds of economic activity.

This is not true to anything like the same extent of manufacturing regions, though it is true of them, also, in degrees that are sometimes quite important. Mining communities are where the minerals are (though by no means *wherever* the minerals are – many known deposits are too remote from good transport to be economically workable), and this means that many of them are a long way from the main concentrations of people and of other economic activity. Agriculture, by the same token, is where the fertile land is, and spreads those engaged in it relatively thinly over large areas. A manufacturing establishment, on the other hand, is less tied down to natural resources, tends to require workers in large numbers to benefit from proximity to similar and complementary activities, and to be attracted by its markets, so that manufacturing is on the whole a 'people-seeking' activity. (So, to an even greater extent, are the service industries.) A further characteristic – implied to some extent by what has just been said – is that manufacturing areas may contain a great variety of industries, and may also change from one principal kind of manufacturing industry to another – or, indeed, to service industries – without any great alteration in their pattern of settlement or general way of life in a way that is much less open to agricultural and mining communities. But we shall see that, in discussing problem-ridden manufacturing areas we are dealing to a disproportionate extent only with those that are exceptions, those which share some of the characteristics of the agricultural and mining problem areas.

'STRUCTURAL' AND 'REGIONAL' FACTORS

Nevertheless, because of the greater versatility of manufacturing regions, a question arises about them which crops up only in a less subtle form about agricultural and mining ones – whether their success, or lack of it, is to be ascribed to the choice of industries they have made or inherited, or to some other factor peculiar to themselves as regions: their location, social climate, attitudes and so on. (With agricultural and mining regions the question is less subtle because the answer is generally plainer: the 'regional' influences are more likely to be assessable from physical conditions and the state of technique, the 'structural' ones from the course of the prices of their products in the national or world market.) We have touched in an earlier chapter on the distinction between 'regional' and 'structural' influences on a region's fortunes; it may, however, be useful to look at it again from a slightly different angle.

It is obvious that a depressed region is a region whose industries are depressed – indeed, the expression can have no other economic meaning. What we are seeking to find out by making our distinction is, to repeat, whether the depression is implicit in the industrial structure of the region, or results from some other circumstance, independent of the industrial structure. The first evidence that comes to mind for structure being to blame is that the industry or industries in which the region specialises are doing badly in all the regions of the country in which they are found. The first practical difficulty, however, is that industries that are in all relevant respects like those in which the region specialises may not, in fact, be found in other regions. Similarly classified industries elsewhere may be quite different – wool textile industries rather than cotton, for instance, both being classified as 'textiles', or steam locomotives rather than motor-cars, both being classed as 'transport equipment'. Even with a much finer classification, one may find that one region specialises, for example, in expensive high-quality products of a particular class, others in mass-produced goods, the market for which may be moving in quite a different way. Unless one is, to a reasonable degree, comparing like with like, evidence of this kind may cast the blame on some unidentified regional factor when it really rests on the region's choice of specialism.

Where one is comparing like with like, evidence of this kind is, *prima facie*, valid. Likewise, if one finds that the industry in which the region specialises – and which is doing badly there – is doing well in all other regions where it is found, then there is *prima facie* reason for looking to the region's location, or its social climate or some other peculiarity as the source of trouble.

In practice, of course, a region is likely to contain many industries, if not specimens of all the kinds distinguished in the industrial classification. Some of them will generally be doing better than similarly described industries elsewhere, some worse; and a given industry is likely to display a considerable range of performances across the different regions where it occurs. As we have already noted in an earlier chapter, therefore, a region may be depressed for any of three reasons:

(1) It may show a systematic tendency to do worse than other regions perhaps in every separate industry, but more generally on a weighted average of their performances (the verdict varying according to the system of weights chosen).

(2) It may show a systematic tendency to specialise in those industries that do badly, judged by their performance either in every single region, or more generally as judged by a weighted average of their performances in different regions (the verdict again varying according to the method of assessment).

(3) It may have specialised in those industries in which its performance in relation to other regions is particularly bad – there may, that is to say, be an inverse correlation between its competitive performance in an industry and the degree to which it specialises in it.

The difference between a region's growth and the national average can, in fact, be partitioned between these three elements, any of which may be either positive or negative. It is plain from what has been said in listing them that there is room for choice in deciding how to measure them. It is not intended here to go deeply into the difficulties this raises, but, briefly, the outcome is as follows. There are two obvious ways of weighting the differences between the regional and national growth rates of different industries to assess the deficiency in industrial growing power of the region which constitutes element 1; one can use weights expressing either the regional or the national relative importance of the industries. Similarly, there are two obvious ways of weighting the differences between the regional and national importances of the industries to assess the differences in growth due to differences in structure, which constitute element 2; one can use as weights either the regional or the national growth rates of the industries. It can be shown that, if one uses national weights in both cases, then element 3 emerges in the form in which it has been described above as the portion of the actual growth difference between the region and the country as a whole which is not accounted for by elements 1 and 2 together. They may be referred to as respectively the 'regional', 'structural' and 'comparative advantage' elements.

Some ways of measuring the first two of these cause the third to vanish – it is, indeed, plain that the third element has something to do both with the region's structure and with its performance in comparison with the rest of the country in particular industries. If, however, it is kept separate and thought of under the name we have given it, it does in fact serve a useful analytical purpose. The theory of comparative advantage tells us that a region or a country is making the most of its opportunities if it specialises in the industries in which it has the greatest advantage over other regions, or the least disadvantage in relation to them. If rate of employment growth can be taken as a measure of the success of an industry in a region, by which it can be compared with that of the same industry in another region, then a positive value of the 'comparative advantage' element serves as an indication that the region is tending to specialise in such a way as to squeeze more growth out of the fact that its industries do not all show the same degree of vigour in relation to their national counterparts.

It is, however, worth noting that, when we are discussing regions which show different rates of growth of employment, we are in territory where the principle of comparative advantage has to be handled with care. The circumstances in which it points the way to the optimal use of resources are those in which the countries concerned have fixed amounts of the factors of production. If labour, for instance, can move freely from one country to another, the recipe for maximum output in a country where labour is absolutely less productive in all industries than that it is in another country is not specialisation in the industry in which its comparative disadvantage is smallest – it is emigration. This should go on to the point where it is possible for productivity to be the same in all industries and in both countries.

In regional economics, we are dealing with a situation where mobility of labour between regions is very considerable, though far from perfect, and where that mobility is, indeed, the necessary condition of much of the inter-regional variation in growth rate of total employment. If a region is achieving a high rate of employment growth by specialising in industries that have a rapid growth rate everywhere – if, that is to say, it has a structure favourable to growth – it is likely to be doing this by drawing immigrants in from other regions; though it *may* happen, coincidentally, that some of its superiority in employment growth is provided by a higher-than-average rate of natural increase in its labour force. If labour is not very mobile between regions, then a region with a favourable industrial structure and only an average rate of natural increase of population will run into labour shortage, and one would expect the rates of growth of its industries to fall below those of their counterparts elsewhere, where labour is less scarce.

What all this means in relation to specialisation and structure is that, given that the mobility of some factors of production between regions is both far from negligible and far from perfect, (1) specialising in the industry in which it has the greatest *comparative* advantage in growth rate (or the least comparative disadvantage) can make a contribution to a region's total employment growth, but (2) a greater one can be made by specialising in the industry which simply has the highest *absolute* growth rate; while (3) the total growth rate, and hence the growth rates of particular industries, that can be achieved in a region, are modified by the frictions that impede its drawing-in of labour and capital from outside.

'STRUCTURAL' AND 'REGIONAL' FACTORS IN PARTICULAR COUNTRIES

There have been a number of studies of the extent to which the structure of manufacturing industry, or of industry in general, can be held responsible for the differences between regional growth rates of manufacturing in a number of countries. Borts and Stein, in their study of regional growth in the United States, found, in two out of three periods for which they performed calculations, no significant correlation between the actual growths of manufacturing employment in states and the hypothetical growth rates which those states would have enjoyed if each of the manufacturing industries had grown in employment everywhere at its national rate. This clearly meant that, for most of the time, the structure of manufacturing industry did not help to provide a general explanation of inter-regional variations in growth rate of total manufacturing employment; the authors point out that it also implies that, where the structure of manufacturing industry was favourable, there must have been a systematic tendency for the industry-by-industry performance to be poor. This is precisely the general tendency that we have referred to in the last paragraph. It does, indeed, seem that regional factors connected with labour supply have been the predominant ones influencing the growth of manufacturing industry in the United States, rather than the composition of that industry. Borts and Stein point out the paradox that, while among states with net immigration of labour into them, the 'regional' element in growth of manufacturing employment was greater the greater that immigration, it was also true that among states with net emigration (i.e. labour surplus) the 'regional' element in the growth of manufacturing was greater than among states with net immigration.

The explanation seems to be that there has been rapid growth of manufacturing in at least two kinds of state – the poor, agricultural states of the south, where indigenous labour was abundant and emigrating, and the relatively empty western states, in which, essentially, the process of colonisation by both labour and capital has been going on. The problem manufacturing areas of slow growth or actual decline have been the old, highly industrialised ones, most notably the textile districts of New England. Through a large part of their history of relative or absolute decline, they, too, must be said to have suffered from regional rather than structural factors, because the textile industries that were declining in them were growing rapidly in the southern states – nationally this was not a declining industry until relatively recently. We shall return to this episode later.

This perhaps serves to bring out an obvious point – that what is 'regional' depends on the extent of the larger, in our context generally the national, frame of reference. 'Structural' influences in the United States emerge as comparatively weak, and 'regional' influences as comparatively strong, largely because it is a very large country with a great diversity of resources, so that what is doing badly in one part of it has a much better chance of doing well in another than is the case when the frame of reference for the depressed region is narrower. It must also be borne in mind that, while there are few manufacturing regions whose particular fortunes can be ascribed, in the American context, mainly to their particular structure, the most important non-manufacturing problem regions of the country, the cotton belt of the south and the coal-mining areas, West Virginia and Pennsylvania, certainly suffer from difficulties that can be described as 'structural'.

France, being a country in which the decline of agricultural employment in favour of secondary and tertiary activities has lately been the most important structural change, also shows the structural elements as the largest components of relative decline in the largely agricultural regions of the west and south-west, and the mining areas, especially the Nord region, also suffer from structural disadvantages, as we have seen. Within manufacturing, the industries with actually declining employment have been textiles, clothing, iron smelting, leather and timber products. At the other end of the scale, the industries of rapidly growing employment are engineering and vehicles, chemicals, plastics and printing. The regions with conspicuously unfavourable structures are Nord, Languedoc and Midi-Pyrénées, and they were among the slowest growers (Nord actually declining) in industrial employment, though the western, agricultural regions did at least as badly in their industrial sectors without the latter having conspicuously unfavourable structures. This latter feature is, clearly, quite different from United States experience in which, as we have seen, the less industrialised regions with manpower surpluses showed rapid industrial growth. The only French region to owe its rapid growth in manufacturing mainly to structural factors is Franche-Comté, with its strength in the motor industry, engineering and plastics. But the most rapid growth of manufacturing employment was, in fact, in the ring of regions surrounding Paris – Picardie, Basse-Normandie, Centre, Bourgogne – where there was no very conspicuous structural advantage but, evidently, a strong locational one.

Thus, structural factors seem to explain an important, though not overwhelming proportion of the cases of stagnant or declining manufacturing regions in France, but little of the incidence of rapid manufacturing growth. When we come to the United Kingdom, structure seems again to have been important, perhaps more so than in France and certainly more so than in the United States. Structure of the economy as a whole, as opposed to manufacturing industry alone, has manifested its influence relatively little through variations in its agricultural component, because agriculture nowhere employs a very large proportion of the active population. But, as we have seen, the incidence of mining employment has been important. So, too, has the concentration in the south-east, East Anglia and the south-west of the rapidly growing services (central government, finance, professional and scientific) and of head-office activities. A similar concentration exists in France, mostly, of course, in the Paris region, but with Provence-Côte d'Azur as an almost equally concentrated small model of it. As between the geographically much larger United States regions, the variation in the proportion of service trades seems to be much less, though at the state level – when we consider Florida, or Hawaii or the District of Columbia and its immediate surroundings – heavy concentration on service activities which are expanding rapidly is a powerful cause of growth beyond the average.

So far as manufacturing is concerned, textiles and ship building have been the industries most responsible for the creation of problem areas in the United Kingdom, since they have fallen rapidly in employment and are also heavily localised. Heavy reliance upon the two together has been a principal cause of the depression of Northern Ireland, the region of slowest growth in the country over the period since 1921 taken as a whole; though an adverse 'regional' factor has been almost as important, and a tendency to do worse relatively to the rest of the country in these particular industries than in others has made a smaller contribution. Heavy reliance upon cotton textiles was the largest cause also of the relative decline of the north-western region; the proportion of total national employment in this industry that

126

the region contained was so high as to make any estimate of a 'regional' disadvantage in it of little significance; though if one works with the broader class of 'textiles' in general, an unfavourable 'regional' factor emerges simply because cotton textiles have declined in national employment faster than others, which are localised in other regions. Of the other regions that relied heavily on textiles, Yorkshire & Humberside and the east midlands, the former has had its growth rate reduced by the decline of the wool textile industry – of which, again, it has almost a national monopoly – while the latter has managed rather better-than-average growth, partly because its textile specialisation is on the knitwear industry which has done better than production of woven textiles, and partly for other reasons.

Ship building, which developed in the late nineteenth century on a highly localised basis mostly in the neighbourhood of coastal iron and steel centres, has been an important factor in the industrial difficulties of Tyneside and the north-east coast, besides Northern Ireland.

Looking rather more generally at the part played by industrial structure in inter-regional variations of prosperity in the United Kingdom, one sees a tendency which we have already noted in France; structure explains a relatively large part of the misfortunes of areas of declining, or slow-growing employment; much less of the good fortune of expanding areas. (This is more strikingly true at the sub-regional than at the regional level.) Regions, or sub-regions, with a heavy reliance on industries that are declining nationally tend to share in that decline, subject always to variations which may amount to differences between what are classified together as portions of the same 'industry'. There is no case of a United Kingdom region that has grown at less than the national average rate without the help (or rather the hindrance) of an unfavourable structural component. On the other hand, some of the regions, and many of the sub-regions, that have done well, have done so not because industrial establishments already in them were expanding or proliferating at something like the rates to be seen nationally in the respective industries, but because they were being 'colonised', usually by both labour and capital, from prosperous regions, perhaps where growth was constrained by local circumstances, or by policy. (In some cases capital was flowing into them from abroad.) This has been notably true, at the regional level, of the south-west and East Anglia, and at the sub-regional level of the sub-regions surrounding Greater London, and some adjacent to other conurbations where space was scarce. In short, expanding industries are apt to initiate movement (usually in the form of the establishment of branches some distance away from their home base); stagnant or contracting industries, naturally, are not. Of course, if the expanding industries in regions of favourable structure always threw out branches into regions of unfavourable structure, the association between the latter and economic decline would be broken, just as effectively as that between favourable structure and expansion. In fact, however, in both the United Kingdom and France, a good deal of the expansion emanating from regions of favourable structure has taken place in neighbouring regions, not the most depressed, and (around Greater London and the Paris Region) it has been manned partly by overspill of population from the metropolis rather than by local labour.

One could go on to consider the contribution of structure to the difficulties of other industrial areas that have not done well (the Walloon area of Belgium, which suffers from declining employment not only in coal mining but also in iron and steel is an obvious example), and perhaps to discuss the reasons for the adverse 'regional' components of deficiency in growth where these appear to be significant. It will, however, perhaps be more useful to pass to the examination in somewhat greater detail of the courses of events in some textile regions which have had difficulties, taking our examples from England, France and the United States. What part of their difficulties was due to location and other 'regional' factors can then be considered rather more usefully, having regard to the part that is, at least *prima facie*, 'structural'.

THE BACKGROUND OF THE TEXTILE INDUSTRIES

Apart from agriculture and coal mining, the textile industries have probably been responsible for more 'structural' regional difficulties than any others. On the world scale, textile production, while an expanding activity, has expanded a great deal less fast than manufacturing as a whole; between 1929 and 1959, for instance, it is reckoned to have increased in output by some 56 per cent, while the world index of total manufacturing production nearly trebled. The income elasticity of demand for both clothing and textile fibres is, on evidence from many countries, apparently well under unity, while that for manufactured goods as a whole is well above unity – in some countries as high as two. This, however, makes the world textile industry a relatively slow-growing, not a declining one, though in early phases of development, with factory production taking over from handicraft production, employment probably fell. What is more important, so far as the advanced countries are concerned, is the great shift, mostly international, in the location of the industry.

The modern textile industries started in the United Kingdom and spread first to other West European countries. Because of the big advantage that these countries possessed in the combination of commercial organisation, capital supply, mechanical knowledge and traditional textile skills that made for successful factory production and marketing, they became suppliers of textiles and textile goods to the rest of the world on a very large scale. Shortly before the First World War, the United Kingdom was exporting about five times as much cotton in manufactured form as she consumed herself, and her exports supplied between a third and a half of the total consumption of factory-made cotton textiles in the world, outside Europe, the United States and Japan. Cotton was the extreme case; but a similar, rather less dramatic, British domination was to be seen in wool. In textiles as a whole, the United Kingdom was responsible for about 46 per cent of world exports, France and Germany (in roughly equal parts) accounting for the greater part of the remainder. The United States was, as in many other products, much more a producer for her own large home market; even in cotton, where her comparative advantage was greatest, her net exports were then, and remained, only a few per cent of her output.

The further spread of textile manufacture changed this picture drastically. Textile production is now as much the leading factory industry in most developing countries as it was in Britain in her industrial revolution. The reasons are partly similar in the two cases. Much textile production under factory conditions requires only relatively modest skills, especially in the fields of design and production engineering. But what is probably more important is the fact that, in a poor country, textiles are the manufactured product consumed in by far the greatest quantity. In the smaller of those countries which, collectively, make up a large part of the less developed world, indeed, simple cotton textiles may be almost the only products in which the demands of the home market are sufficient to support even one factory unit large enough to employ the modern methods of the developed parts of the world. The industry is, therefore, the one which grows best under the shelter of a moderate amount of protection.

The result of this was twofold. First, world trade in textiles which had risen by about a third in the first fourteen years of this century, rose no higher in the decade after the First World War, and declined in the subsequent twenty years to something like its level at the beginning of the century. (It began to rise again from 1950, and has continued to rise, though considerably less rapidly, proportionately, than production.) Second, the roles of the trading countries changed. British exports, measured at constant prices, had already, in 1929, fallen by a third below their peak value of 1913, and proceeded to fall by rather more than a quarter from then to the eve of the Second World War. There was a brief postwar remission of the trend, but by 1955 the figure was down to some 28 per cent of the 1913 peak. French and German experience repeated this pattern in less pronounced degrees. German textile exports reached their first peak (at constant prices) before the First World War, as did British, and, by 1955, though recovering rapidly from their virtual cessation in the Second World War, were still 25 per cent below that peak. French exports reached their peak about 1929, and in 1955 were below the peak level by about a third.

The place of these old exporters was taken by new ones; mainly by Japan, whose exports reached their peak on the eve of the Second World War, though also by Italy, Belgium and Switzerland, while India showed a steady growth of exports from the beginning of the century onwards. Latterly, the most rapidly expanding exports have been those from a variety of developing countries, including Hong Kong, Taiwan, Portugal and Korea.

THE NORTH-WEST REGION

The classic area of former expansion and subsequent decline in the textile industry is the cotton textile area of north-western England. In 1912, the direct employment in the industry there was well over 600,000, nearly a quarter of the total labour force of this large industrial area with an aggregate population of over 5 million. Four-fifths of its production was exported, and these exports still constituted nearly three-fifths of total international trade in cotton manufactures. By 1973, the number employed in the industry in the region was down to 144,000, about 5 per cent of the regional total. The biggest absolute decline in employment came in the first phase of the contraction, before the Second World War. It was accompanied by severe unemployment. Already in 1924, when the number in employment had shrunk by 120,000 from its pre-1914 peak, the number of unemployed described as members of the industry's labour force was 73,000. By 1930, when the number in work had shrunk by a further 143,000, over 200,000 were unemployed. At its highest, in 1931, the percentage of the insured labour force unemployed (in all industries together) in the north-western region stood at 28·2 per cent: the highest in that year for any United Kingdom region except Wales – the depression had, of course, brought severe unemployment in other industries besides cotton textiles, as well as accentuating the decline of the latter industry. By 1938, the number of unemployed associated with the industry had halved, to 100,000, though employment stood some 70,000 below its 1930 level at less than half of what it had been in 1912. The industry's labour force, employed and unemployed together, shrank only slowly in the 1920s; the big fall took place in the depressed thirties. It continued as a result of 'concentration' in the industry and the high demand for labour in more closely war-related activities during the following years, and employment at the end of the Second World War stood at only just over 200,000, with unemployment practically nonexistent. There followed the boom of 1945–51, in which foreign competition was greatly reduced through the disorganisation of continental European and Japanese industry, and demand, augmented by the emptiness of wardrobes after the years of wartime shortage, was very high. Employment rose by some 50 per cent; in the course of the succeeding twenty years, it halved.

Both before and after the Second World War, the north-west has managed to maintain an expanding trend in its total employment; in both periods this has been the result of a falling trend in its 'basic' industries (taken together) – those producing goods and services not of the kinds that are necessarily consumed locally – and a rising trend in the (mostly service) industries that sell in the local market. In both periods its growth has been much slower than that of the country as a whole, though it has not been the slowest-growing region in Great Britain – Scotland has achieved that unenviable distinction since the war, and Wales, with an absolute fall in employment, achieved it before. In both periods, too, it has shown considerable net emigration, equal to about two-thirds of its natural increase of population between the wars and about a third of it more recently, its natural increase being, in both periods, somewhat slower than the national average. The great difference between the two periods, however, has been in the level of unemployment. Since 1945, the north-west's unemployment rate, while fairly consistently above the national average, has only rarely and briefly been much above it, and that, of course, means that, by prewar standards it has been low. Indeed, whereas the earlier contraction was marked by severe unemployment, the more recent one has been accompanied mostly by labour shortage in the textile industry; this has been given by industrialists as a reason for their not expanding production at times when demand was strong, as in the mid-sixties.

As the rate of change in the industrial structure has not been very different since the war from what it was before, perhaps all one can say about the great difference in the incidence of unemployment in the north-west is that, like the corresponding national difference, it results from the difference in the pressure of effective demand. If so, it illustrates strikingly how powerful such a difference can be in altering the unemployment rate, even in a situation where rapid change in the structure of demand might be expected to keep it at some very substantial minimum level.

NORTH-EAST LANCASHIRE

From this very general survey of experience in the north-western region during the decline of the cotton textile industry there, it may be useful to turn to what has happened in a particular sub-region, on which that decline bore with exceptional force, the weaving area of north-east Lancashire. The localisation of the cotton industry in the north-west is a most striking phenomenon. Not only was some 90 per cent of the British cotton textile industry, at its peak, concentrated in this region, but it was largely confined to its eastern margin, to the foothills of the Pennines and their outliers, and did not spill out on to the quite broad coastal plain. This localisation within the region is generally explained by reference to the importance for the industry, in its formative period in the late eighteenth and early nineteenth centuries, of access to soft water for the bleaching, dyeing and printing processes, and to power in the form first of hill streams, later of coal. It was also, no doubt, a matter of comparative advantage – where agriculture could be prosperous as a full-time

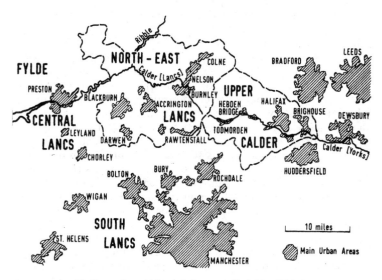

North-east Lancashire and the upper Yorkshire Calder

occupation, textile working did not arise; where it was needed to supplement a poor and seasonal farming life, it did.

But within the textile area there is a further localisation: spinning to the south, weaving to the north. The prevailing explanation of this is that, as spinning was mechanised earlier, it tended to grow most strongly as a factory industry in the part of the range nearest to the point of entry of the raw material, namely, Liverpool. When, from about 1840 onwards, weaving was becoming mechanised, it found its location in the more distant parts, where there were already many handloom weavers, and where there was less competition for the predominantly rural recruits to the labour force. But whatever the reason, there was certainly a progressive concentration of weaving in towns that grew quickly in the second half of the nineteenth century along the valleys of the southern tributaries of the Ribble, and grew up dependent upon the single activity of cotton weaving to a most unusual extent. It was still true in 1930 (though one must remember that insurance against unemployment was less comprehensive then than now) that 70 per cent of the insured workers in Burnley were in the cotton industry, and the proportion (on the more comprehensive modern definitions) was 44 per cent as late as 1953.

Not only was the weaving area more highly specialised in its principal industry than the spinning area (and, *a fortiori*, than the region as a whole), but that principal industry suffered a more severe blow. Weaving is a less capital-intensive activity than spinning, and tends to be established ahead of it in developing countries. Demand for Lancashire woven goods fell more drastically than that for yarn, because the export trade in the latter held up better. Output fell by 60 per cent between 1912 and 1937–8, whereas the fall in yarn production was only some 40 per cent. Between 1921 and 1938, the population of the spinning area fell by about 3 per cent, but that of the weaving area, on a fairly restrictive definition of its boundaries, fell by almost 13 per cent, a cumulative fall of 0·8 per cent a year. The rate of decline in the weaving area slowed down subsequently, until it turned into a modest increase in the later sixties; that in the spinning area appears to have turned the corner by the fifties. The main weaving area – the standard sub-region of north-east Lancashire – thus shows a continuous history of population-decline from about 1911 to 1966, a decline of some 20 per cent over that fifty-five-year period.

As in the north-western region as a whole, the contrast between the rates of unemployment that accompanied the earlier and the later phases of this contraction is very sharp. In the eleven years 1926–36, unemployment among insured persons in the Blackburn area (the largest centre of the weaving district) averaged 33·5 per cent, about half as great again as in the region as a whole. In the fifties and sixties, the general level was not greatly different from that of the whole region, though somewhat more volatile. The great feature of north-east Lancashire from the war until very recently has been, not unemployment, but decline in both total and occupied population.

Part of the reason for the population decline was slow, almost negligible, net natural increase. Low fertility has been characteristic of the English textile areas generally for a century or more. The north-western region also has a standardised mortality rate considerably (currently some 10 per cent) above the national average. Mainly, no doubt, from a combination of these reasons, the sub-region has long shown natural increase about 0·5 per cent a year below the national average. In the thirties and the fifties, there was a net natural decrease. But net outward migration has been generally more important. In the thirties, the sub-region lost more than 1 per cent of its population annually by net outward migration, though by the sixties this rate had been reduced to a fifth or a sixth of that high value.

Both before and after the Second World War, the fall in employment in the sub-region seems to have been rather larger, proportionately, than that in resident population. In part, this is no doubt due to the retirement from the labour force of some people – mostly women – who, in the absence of closures in the textile industry, would have remained occupied. We shall return to this point presently. In addition, it may be due to a change in the balance and extent of daily travel to work. There is an appreciable net outflow of daily commuters, mainly to the Preston area to the west, and it seems that this has increased. The tendency for there to be net outward movement in this direction is no doubt encouraged by the existence of a very appreciable differential of average earnings in comparable occupations between north-east and central Lancashire, to the disadvantage of the former. The tendency to commute outwards to work elsewhere as an alternative to moving house is likely to be strengthened by the low level of rents and house prices in the sub-region, though against this has to be set the high average age of much of the accommodation available, and various other disadvantages of environment. On the whole, however, the striking thing is the smallness of net outward commuting from this sub-region, in comparison with the very considerable daily movements between different local authority areas within it.

Mention has been made of the change in the proportion of women who are members of the workforce. This proportion (the female 'activity rate' or 'participation rate') has traditionally been high in British textile areas, and, since the Second World War, it has generally been rising throughout the country, fastest where it was initially lowest. It is noteworthy that the north-west was the only region in which it showed a declining trend in the period 1954–64, though it cannot be said that the extent of decline was statistically significant. The north-east Lancashire sub-region in 1971 still showed the highest female activity rate within the region, and one of the two or three highest of any sub-region in the United Kingdom. It had not changed significantly in the previous five years. It seems, therefore, that employment opportunities for those women who remained in the sub-region had been pretty well maintained; the worst that can be said is that they did not share the improvement that occurred in most of the rest of the country. This is perhaps the more surprising in view of the fact that these opportunities in north-east Lancashire suffered a double blow; not only was the great traditional employer of women – the weaving industry – in rapid decline, but, within it, the relative part played by men was increasing, with the growth of automation (which raised the proportionate importance of maintenance as compared with process workers), and with the growth of shift working, women being excluded from night shifts.

Insofar, therefore, as employment opportunities in the sub-region have shrunk, it is the low (for a long time negative) rate of natural increase and the substantial net outward migration that have mostly been responsible for adjusting the resident population to this shrinkage. These two factors are not independent of one another, because neither emigrants from an area nor immigrants into it are usually the same in age and sex composition (and therefore in their impact on birth and death rates) as the resident population as a whole. Very commonly, both emigrants and immigrants are young adults, some of them with children. If, therefore, emigration exceeds immigration, the result is to depress birth rates and raise death rates – slow growth of the population seems to be partly attributable to low natural increase, but this low natural increase is, in turn, partly due to the net emigration.

This was certainly true of north-east Lancashire, though with the qualification that an unusually high proportion of the emigrants are of retirement age. The climate of the area is not kind to the elderly, whereas that of the nearby Lancashire coast is, and the track to it is a well-beaten one. The low birth rate of the sub-region in the last generation is largely explained by the high emigration among those who at the relevant time were in the most fertile age-groups, or of their parents. It was not, incidentally, predominantly textile workers who emigrated, nor to any large extent the unemployed, at least in the more recent years; as is common elsewhere, the incidence of emigration has been high among professional and scientific workers and public servants, but also, in this case, among engineering workers. As is also common, at least in the United Kingdom, a high proportion of those leaving the sub-region did not go very far – over half of them were dispersed over the rest of the north-western region (including an eighth, presumably mainly the elderly, who went to the Fylde); about an eighth went to the neighbouring Yorkshire region, and another eighth to the great magnet of the south-east. As to the reasons given by emigrants for their moves, it is noteworthy that climate and environment were mentioned by nearly half a sample questioned in 1967 – nearly as many as mentioned work opportunities, though work was much more important as the *main* reason for moving.

Immigrants, not surprisingly, declare themselves motivated mainly by work opportunities, next by family reasons, and hardly at all by environment and climate; but, in a minor but perhaps significant number of cases by the ready availability of housing in this area of net population loss.

Much of this is in accordance with what is known about the motives for internal movement over more than trivial distances in the United Kingdom generally. It is not (or not to the extent one would perhaps expect) those thrown out of work in a declining industry who make up the majority of migrants; it is those receiving or seeking promotion, the better-educated, those in expanding industries. Those moving for family reasons presumably tend to reinforce other tendencies, to accompany or follow other migrants on balance. Climate and environment are substantial secondary reasons for movement in some cases,

137

increasingly as standards of life and expectations rise.

Those who move out for any reason will in many cases create employment opportunities, some of which will be filled, directly or indirectly, by the local unemployed, but a *net* outward movement also has adverse local multiplier effects. Even if the immediate effect is only to reduce the number of the unemployed, local tradesmen and others suffer from the net loss of the local expenditure generated by the relevant unemployment and supplementary benefits. But in north-east Lancashire the urge to move out seems to have been especially strong, so that, for the weaving industry at least, an actual shortage of labour was created in more recent years. Between 1966 and 1971 a new factor emerged – the population decline of the sub-region was reversed. The size of the labour force is not yet affected by this, of course, but the long-term outlook is. At present it remains a phenomenon rather hard to explain.

What this appears to mean is that, after a traumatic period between the two World Wars, when unemployment was very high, north-east Lancashire has achieved a fairly complete adjustment. Partly, as we have seen, this was because the heavy net emigration of the thirties produced a longer-continuing reduction of natural population increase; partly it seems to have been because the heavy net emigration removed labour directly; partly because of its effect in reducing the rate of natural increase of population. The emigration was heaviest when unemployment was very high, but it continued at a reduced rate through the later years when low earnings and the perception of limited opportunities in a declining industry, rather than actual unemployment, must have provided the main economic motive for leaving. It was assisted by environmental factors. In this sub-region where a very high proportion of the buildings were erected before the beginning of the present century, the effect of a built environment looking (as in much of Lancashire and the West Riding) as if it had recently been bombed, and of considerable industrial air pollution, is reinforced by the heavy cloud-cover and rainfall that characterise the western foothills of the Pennines. It is not an area that lacks the normal urban amenities, nor can it be regarded as very remote from bigger centres, but it cannot claim either metropolitan or rural attractions in degrees to compensate for these disadvantages. In these circumstances, the net outward movement from it has something in common with that from some agricultural districts; the preference for

138

other surroundings, together with the effect of market forces on relative earnings, is sufficient to keep the supply of labour down at least to the demand for it in the area where that demand is falling.

The growth of demand outside the cotton industry has, however, naturally also played a part. One component of this growth, common to the whole country (indeed, to all advanced economies) is that for labour in the service industries. In the United Kingdom, the general tendency has been for the balance of employment to be shifted from primary production and manufacturing to service trades which are mainly local or regional in the market they serve. This is the result of changes in the structure of demand and in the technology by which it is satisfied. A region with a fixed number employed in the former (non-regional or 'basic') group of industries would, broadly, tend to increase the number in the remaining, 'regional' industries by about 0·5 per cent a year of its *total* employment. In addition, any extra employment in its basic industries would tend to be accompanied by an increase in that of its 'regional' industries about three-quarters as great.

North-east Lancashire should, according to this formula, have shown a slight fall in its service employment, since employment in manufacturing, mining and agriculture fell, in the postwar period, fast enough to offset the independent shift towards service industries. In fact, service employment increased slightly. The supply of labour (especially female labour) available in the area must have attracted some service activities of more than local significance. The increased employment in the service trades was, indeed, entirely due to growth of female employment in them.

In manufacturing, the growth of non-textile employment since the war has been equal to only about 40 per cent of the fall in textile employment (it was much less before). The war brought the first substantial impulse towards substitution of new manufacturing activities for old, and some of the metal-working establishments then set up persisted afterwards. Others came in subsequently, most notably in the years 1953–60 when parts of the sub-region benefited from incentives provided by the government as part of its regional policy. The indigenous textile-machinery industry provided a useful base for the mainly engineering activities that developed, though most of the latter were carried out by branches of firms whose headquarters were elsewhere. The availability of cheap factory space, abandoned by the textile industry, was a considerable attraction, as it was throughout all the textile areas of the north-west. Although the metal-working establishments of the area are not very closely integrated by trade connections with each other, or with industry in the rest of the region, they are not understood to find themselves considerably handicapped by remoteness from markets, suppliers or other essential contacts. The sub-region, though in a somewhat hill-bound fringe of the great industrial belt of the southern Pennines, is reasonably accessible from that belt and its environs as a whole, except in connection with heavy industrial products, with which it does not in fact deal. Perhaps its chief drawback, as a location for the development of manufacturing industry, is the relative scarcity of available level sites. On the whole, apart from its major structural problem, its decline is perhaps attributable marginally more to its unattractiveness to residents, as such, than to its inconvenience for industrialists.

As a footnote, it may be useful to add that the neighbouring area to the east, on the opposite slope of the Pennines, presents some interesting parallels. The upper valley of the (Yorkshire) Calder is another very old textile district, in this case devoted mainly to wool, though to a subsidiary extent to cotton, and it has some other substantial industries, including machine tools, carpets and food products. Its population, now just under 200,000, has declined gently and steadily since 1901 – by about 15 per cent in 70 years. This decline is not so obviously connected with that of the Yorkshire wool textile, industry as a whole, which has been going on since the First World War, but has been far less dramatic than the disasters of Lancashire cotton. Indeed, the earlier shrinkage of the population of these narrow valleys was more a matter of the superior attractions to industry of the larger wool textile centres farther east than of any general industrial decline. The paradoxical feature of the more recent situation – a paradox not yet presented quite so clearly in north-east Lancashire – is the coexistence of very low unemployment, considerable labour shortage, high activity rates, and the daily importation by firms of women workers from the south Yorkshire coalfield, thirty miles away, with continued net emigration at a rate latterly not very different from that experienced on the other side of the watershed.

The key to this seems to lie in the evidence (though it is not very complete) that earnings in the area are low. That this should be so in a situation of labour shortage itself requires explanation. It is probably the case that the main industry, as in north-east Lancashire, finds itself in the weak competitive position associated with rising competition elsewhere, and simply cannot afford to pay more. It is a situation probably commonest in industries where trade union organisation is relatively weak (or, at least, not very aggressive), which includes many with a high reliance upon female labour. In these cases, save where the upsurge of competition or the collapse of demand is very severe, establishments are not forced into closure by inability to sell their products; it is in the labour market that they are gradually outbid. As industrial deaths go, it must be reckoned a happy one.

THE NORTHERN FRENCH TEXTILE AREA

The decline of employment in the French textile industries has posed less severe problems than that in the United Kingdom, because the industries in question were smaller in relation to total employment and less heavily localised. Both of these circumstances are connected in some degree with the fact that industrialisation came so much later in France; the United Kingdom got in first as the supplier of cheap, mass-produced textile goods to a large part of the world, and France consequently did not achieve a position of such high dependence upon export trade as that from which the UK was displaced by overseas industrialisation from 1914 onwards. At its peak, the United Kingdom had nearly 1,400,000 people occupied in the textile trades; France had not many more than half that number. French textile exports at their peak in the late 1920s were not much more than a fifth (at constant prices) of what British had been at their peak just before the First World War.

The lower degree of localisation in France also can be attributed, at least in part, to the later and slower industrialisation in the nineteenth century, the age in which that process seems to have produced a degree of local specialisation not matched before or since. Much of the British pattern of localisation seems to have been determined in the fifty or seventy years before 1850, when industry was becoming dependent upon power, but that power was not cheaply conveyable far from its physical source. It was in this period that British development was running ahead of French. There was little tendency (except perhaps in Alsace and Lorraine) for French textile industry to become established in relatively remote sites which happened to have water-power. For these, and no doubt many other reasons, neither the cotton nor the wool textile industry in France has ever been concentrated overwhelmingly in one district, as happened in England, and the French scene is further diversified by the presence of the large silk industry (and other trades related to it) in the Rhone valley, where it owed its establishment initially to suitability for growing mulberry trees.

In the end (or rather, at the peak of activity), therefore, there came to be a number of French textile districts. The Lille-Roubaix-Tourcoing district (Nord département) on the Belgian border, working in both wool and cotton, must have achieved a peak textile employment of about 200,000 – somewhat less than the comparable figure for the West Riding of Yorkshire, and only a third of the peak figure for cotton in Lancashire. The Lyons district, with textile employment about equal to three-quarters of that in the Nord département, comes second; then come Alsace and Lorraine, each less than a third as big as the Nord in textile employment, followed by some five scattered centres each with employment in the 25,000–45,000 range.

It has already been remarked that the smaller degree of French dependence on exports in comparison with the United Kingdom made for a lower degree of vulnerability. It is, nevertheless, true that the French textile industry suffered a severe shock in the depression of the thirties. Exports were some 60 per cent lower in 1937 than in 1929 and production some 12 per cent lower. Between 1931 and 1936, total employment fell by 13·5 per cent in the Nord region. Indeed, industrial production and employment altogether in France were seriously depressed in the later thirties; employment 9 per cent lower in 1936 than in 1931. The consequences of this do not show to more than a small extent in the unemployment statistics: those statistics are not satisfactory as measures of involuntary idleness, and it is likely that, as in previous hard times, a fair proportion of those who lost their jobs in industry disappeared into the countryside. Postwar recovery, however, brought production (though not employment) in textiles some 20 per cent above the immediate prewar level by the mid-fifties, and it is from then that the more serious and better-documented decline dates.

In the Nord département, this decline was, however, rather slower than that in Lancashire. Between 1954 and 1968, textile employment fell by 51,000, or nearly a third (against more than

142

half in a slightly longer period in the Lancashire cotton area). This fall amounted to about 13 per cent of all jobs in 1954 in the département's secondary industry.

The impact of this on the Nord département's economy compares in an interesting way with that of parallel events on the British textile districts. There are very important differences between the textile industries in the two countries. For one thing, the dependence upon female labour in France is much smaller than in England – perhaps a reflection of the fact that France has always possessed a relatively large reserve of male labour in her countryside. Dependence upon women employees in industry as a whole is not, moreover, showing the sharply increasing trend that is evident in the United Kingdom, probably for the same reason. Secondly, the main reserves of labour are not to be found among the recorded unemployed; the latter fluctuate in numbers very much less than the numbers in employment. This, in the United Kingdom, is true of women, and is true to a much smaller extent of men – with the latter it is most noticeable in the regions where demand for labour is high – but in France it seems, at least until the seventies, to have been true generally and to a very striking extent. From the mid-fifties, with the decline in textile employment, the total numbers in employment of all kinds in the Nord département increased very much less than the total population. This was attributable only to a relatively small extent to changes in age composition; for the most part it was due to a rise in the proportion who were inactive (according to census evidence) in every age-group; yet the rise in the number of recorded unemployed was relatively trivial.

Another important difference from British conditions is the fact that the main French textile area – the Nord département – has traditionally shown a rate of natural increase much above that for France as a whole. (The low rate of natural increase in the British textile areas has often been attributed largely to the high proportion of married women who are in employment there.) This has been mainly responsible for preventing any fall in population in the Nord département in the recent period of textile decline, though there seems to have been such a fall in the depression of the thirties. But some contribution to this end was also made by the still higher rate of natural increase in the neighbouring, largely coal-mining, département of Pas-de-Calais, which showed one of the most rapid net emigrations of any département – about 0·6 per cent a year – and which appears to have provided a net flow to the Nord next door. At all events, the Nord département, in spite of the decline of its largest industry, showed not only a substantial increase in total population, but also, at least in the sixties, an absence of net outward migration.

One very important circumstance which helps to explain the discrepancy between fairly rapid growth of total resident population and slow growth of total employment in the area is the remarkably large extent to which this textile district relied upon labour commuting into it daily – in the mid-fifties, something approaching 30,000 workers (largely women) from the Pas-de-Calais coalfield to the south, and a further substantial number over the frontier from Belgium. At least a third of the reduction in employment in the textile industry of the area may well be accounted for by reduction in this daily commuting, a factor which may help to explain why it is from the Pas-de-Calais, not from the Nord, that the heavy net emigration has taken place. The contribution of change in the commuting pattern to the adjustment to reduced labour demand is clearly much greater here than it was in north-east Lancashire – basically because the French textile district in question lies near to a large heavy industry area with exceptionally little demand for female workers. (Something of the same kind can be seen in Yorkshire, but there the decline of textile employment has been a more gradual one.) The result, as we have noted, is to shift the burden of change.

But, the striking fact about the Nord département is that its employment, in total, has grown. The growth has been largely in service trades. As we have noted already, the number of jobs in the textile industries fell by 51,000 between 1954 and 1968; jobs in other manufacturing industry at the same time increased by some 17,500 (a modest increase of about 7 per cent), so that total manufacturing employment fell by 8 per cent, but service employment grew by over 94,000 – a proportionate growth of nearly 27 per cent. It must be remembered that agricultural employment had fallen by 42,000, so that the growth in total employment over the fourteen years was only 19,000 (2 per cent); indeed, up to 1962 there had been a slight fall.

The concentration of employment growth in the service sector of the economy has been characteristic of France as a whole, as, indeed, of all the EEC countries; only in Eire and Italy has there been a more than marginal growth in the proportion of the employed population that is in manufacturing, and in the already highly industrialised countries – Belgium and the United Kingdom – there has been a fall. The strong growth of the service sector in France can perhaps be regarded as springing from rapid urbanisation in a country with a high standard of living. The rise in the service population in the Nord département, at about 0·5 per cent of the total occupied population per year, has been a little slower than in France as a whole, and not out of line with British experience. The big gainers, absolutely, as in the country as a whole, have been commerce and finance and public service.

None of the other main textile regions of France was so heavily dependent on that industry in 1954 as the Nord département was. In the succeeding fourteen years, they all suffered declines in textile employment, the largest of which was 50 per cent, in Alsace. All, however, managed, unlike the Nord, to increase their total manufacturing employment, though Lorraine only did so marginally.

NEW ENGLAND

The course in this century of the traditional textile industries in the United States is different from that in other industrial countries in that the decline in employment in them in the country as a whole has been only very moderate; the main event has been a shift of location. New England, an old industrial area, lost the bulk of the industry to the agricultural problem area of the southeast, for which it provided (as we have already noted in Chapter 4) the crucial start in industrialisation. The United States is big enough to show in microcosm the worldwide shift of textile manufacture from the developed to the developing countries.

The textile industries of New England developed originally in ways not very different from those of the United Kingdom. The first factories were early enough to be worked by water rather than steam-power, which meant that they were located inland, on fairly swiftly flowing streams – notably the Connecticut and Merrimack rivers. As steam-power became more important, mostly after the middle of the nineteenth century, the centre of gravity, of the cotton industry especially, moved to coastal centres, notably Fall River and New Bedford in southern Massachusetts, and the neighbouring parts of Rhode Island, though the older inland centres in many cases went on growing. Wool textile manufacture shared many sites with cotton, but was rather more widely dispersed geographically. Like the Pennine textile industries, the New England industries grew and prospered

New England textile areas

146

where they did partly because local agricultural opportunities were too poor to compete successfully with them for manpower.

In these circumstances, some very high degrees of local dependence upon the industry developed. In 1907, it accounted for as much as 85 per cent of all manufacturing employment, (about a third of all employment) in New Bedford, and for much higher proportions, up to perhaps two-thirds, in some other towns, such as Manchester, New Hampshire. The scale of total textile employment in New England also grew large; some 440,000 by 1919, which was well over half the national total. The dependence on international trade (unlike that of Lancashire, for instance, at the same period) was small, but the dependence on markets in other regions of the United States was necessarily high.

From the end of the First World War onwards, there began the rapid growth of textile production in the south-east, to which reference has already been made. Even in the prosperous twenties, this growth was in part at the expense of New England, where both textile and total manufacturing employment began to decline. The largest part of the absolute decline came in the 1930s, to the accompaniment of general depression (in Lancashire, it will be remembered, it came before 1929), and by 1940 employment was down to 257,000. By then, nearly twice this number were employed in the south-east. The New England industry recovered slightly up to the late forties, but from that point there came a precipitous fall of employment to some 124,000 in 1960. In this period, the fifties, textile employment in the United States as a whole, as in the other older manufacturing countries, lost ground before foreign competition; but in the sixties it began to expand again. New England, however, continued to lose textile jobs at an annual rate much the same as before.

There does not seem to be much mystery about the mechanism of the New England loss of the textile industry to the south-east. The most obvious attraction of the cotton belt to entrepreneurs lay in its lower labour costs. In the twenties, New England was still among the high-income areas of the United States, and the south-east showed average personal incomes lower by almost half. Differences in wages were less dramatic, but still substantial. The gap has narrowed over time; hourly earnings in the immediate postwar years, in textile manufacture, seem, however, to have been 15–20 per cent lower in the south than in New England, although for some skilled trades the differences were much smaller. It is true that per capita productivity was initially considerably lower in the south, but by the early fifties the difference seems generally to have been small; indeed, in some cases it was reversed by the greater willingness of southern labour to accept innovations. The south had also some advantages in transport costs and in taxation, though these were probably relatively small factors.

At all events, the industry migrated south. An important factor in its doing so, however, was the success of New England in developing other industries, without which New England wage levels would no doubt have fallen farther in relation to those elsewhere. In fact, the course of events seems to have illustrated the results of the general tendency of labour mobility within a region to even out earnings between industries. The bad times in the locally important textile industries apparently tended to depress wages in other industries also, with the result that the region showed expansion in the generally high-wage metal-fabricating industries (where its wages were well below the national average) and also in the clothing trade, which showed a tendency to come in from the neighbouring high-wage Middle Atlantic states as their labour became dearer in relation to that of New England.

The textile industries thus faced, at least for a time, keener competition for labour in New England than in the south – in the former they are held to have been left with the less able and enterprising, while in the latter they had the pick of trainable (though not trained) labour. What it amounts to is that New England, like other old textile areas in developed countries, had lost a comparative advantage in the industry, dating from a time when conditions were very different. From the fifties onwards, it was becoming plain that the region's new comparative advantage might lie in the light, science-based industries.

The changes in question did not come about without very considerable unemployment. The US Bureau of Employment Security in the fifties listed seventeen major labour markets as chronic labour surplus areas, the test being that they had shown unemployment rates at least 50 per cent above the national average for at least the previous five years. Five of these were New England textile areas – Fall River, Lawrence, Lowell, and New Bedford in Massachusetts, and Providence, Rhode Island. The median of their annual rates in this period was about 10 per cent of the labour force, with a range from 6 per cent to nearly 24 (the latter for Lawrence in 1954). All of these areas except

Providence are labour markets for moderate size – populations around 100,000 – and Providence is a centre of over three-quarters of a million. Their considerable size (in comparison with the very many small and relatively isolated towns of the United States) probably worked in favour of their acquiring new industry, though it is to be noted that some of the small centres dependent on the wool textile industry (which began to decline seriously in New England only in the fifties) were devoted to specialities of high quality, which survived well.

The effects of closures of large mills in small towns were in some cases devastating, though there are also cases in which efforts by the local community succeeded in attracting new industry to take the place of closing textile enterprises, as most notably at Manchester, New Hampshire, in 1935 and Nashua in 1948.

The general buoyancy of the American economy since the war, however, enabled adjustment to take place with little fall in manufacturing employment as a whole; it was only in Rhode Island, in the fifties, that any considerable reduction took place. The New England manufacturing economy is now basically a varied one, with considerable concentration, built up over a long period, on the metal-fabricating industries, and on others that have grown rapidly. The military and aerospace expenditure of the sixties had a powerful effect there, and the Boston area, in particular, became a centre of research and development activity. This growth spread its influence widely over the region. Moreover, as elsewhere, the growth of service employment was greater than that in manufacturing – roughly twice as great as the growth of the non-textile manufacturing industries as a whole. The post-war experience of New England should also be viewed in the light of the fact that (though to a smaller extent than Lancashire) it shows a lower rate of natural increase of population than the national economy of which it forms a part. In the sixties, the region as a whole showed a small net immigration, though the states where textile employment had been largest, Massachusetts and Rhode Island, were still losing over a quarter of their natural increase through a net emigration rate of about 0·25 per cent.

CONCLUSION

All this, once again, as with the other kinds of problem area we have discussed, is hard to summarise, because cases differ greatly from each other. Perhaps the main impression that the recent history of textile districts in the main industrial countries leaves is a confirmation of the presumption with which this chapter started – that a large industrial centre in a modern economy is a durable entity, capable of adapting to seemingly catastrophic declines in its main industry. The second impression, which also reinforces one that might have been derived from our agricultural and mining examples, is that the speed of adaptation is highly sensitive to the general pressure of demand in the economy – or rather, the pressure of demand allied with the rate of growth. The two can be independent, inasmuch as an economy is in principle capable of operating with even some excess of aggregate demand and little growth, because consumption is high and saving and investment low. If there is little investment, the rate of change in the economic structure must be low, and if external demand for some product falls, capital shortage will not permit new enterprises to take the place of those that are made redundant; workers thrown out of employment will have to find work in existing industries which, if the stricken export industry is highly localised, may mean moving to another part of the country. Indeed, it might be claimed that absence of investment in comparison with, say, Germany, France, or (in the sixties) the United States, rather than low general pressure of demand, was what made structural change in the United Kingdom more sluggish than that elsewhere; though the task of adjustment in our chosen case of Lancashire was certainly a large one.

Another point, which is one for further study rather than for firm conclusions from the data presented here, concerns the part played by the price of labour in these changes. We have seen *prima facie* evidence that labour market forces worked strongly in the United States, not only in shifting the textile industry in the first place, but in lowering New England wage rates and thus bringing new enterprise in. The workings of wage differentials in north-east Lancashire and the neighbouring Yorkshire Calder valley seem to have been more modest, and less effective in attracting new industry – perhaps because so much British industry (at any rate in nationwide, multi-plant enterprises) reckons on the necessity of paying something like national rates, even in an area where the offer price of labour might be lower. If this is so, it would suggest that mobility (or the choice between mobility and unemployment) is to some extent forced upon labour by a rigid wage structure. At all events, international comparisons raise more questions than can be easily answered.

150

CHAPTER 7

Agglomerations and Congested Regions in Advanced Countries

The presumption on the part of policy makers and the public that some regions are not developing fast enough, and need to be helped, is often, though not always, accompanied by the presumption that others are in some sense growing too fast, and ought to be held back. Often, the latter regions are described as 'congested'. It is a term which does not always convey exactly what is meant, and in any case demands some further inspection.

SENSES OF 'CONGESTION'

In its most ordinary, everyday meaning, congestion in a region implies the presence in it of too many people, so that the working of that region's economy, or conditions of life in it, are less satisfactory than they would be with a smaller population. But this leaves two matters unsettled. First, is the region as a whole congested, or does congestion exist in only a *part* of the region, so that internal redistribution might remove it? Second, is the superfluity of people the result of limitation of some part (or of all) of the regional stock of capital, so that housing, or water supply, or the transport network is inadequate – a deficiency which is presumably remediable through further investment? Or is the trouble of a more permanent nature? Is the population excessive in relation to the physical extent and natural resources and amenities of the region, to such an extent that, even with more roads, housing and so on in the congested region, it would still be better if some of its people and economic activity were moved to another region? To put it more briefly, one should be clear, first, whether what is alleged is congestion *in* a region, or congestion *of* the region as a whole and, second, whether the congestion has the nature of a temporary bottleneck, or of a

151

permanent maldistribution, even allowing for the long-term possibilities of development.

The former of these questions is important because it is against cities (or, more generally, highly urbanised areas) that the accusation of congestion is mostly, and most plausibly, made, and very often these account for only a fraction of the area of the region that contains them – using 'region', as we have done, to refer to a major division of a country. The south-eastern and north-western regions of England are by far the most densely inhabited regions of one of the most densely inhabited countries in the world, containing, between them, not much less than half the English population, and both have nearly two-thirds of their total area in agricultural use. This statistic of course, depends on the way in which regional boundaries are drawn, but any scheme of division that cut up an advanced country into regions dominated by major concentrations of population would produce a similar effect – closely built-up areas are only small parts, in acreage, of the regions that look to those built-up areas as centres of services and, to a large extent, of employment and supplies. To allow that London or Manchester or Liverpool, is a congested conurbation, therefore, is not necessarily to concede that the south-east, or the north-west, is a congested region.

URBAN CONGESTION AND SIZE

We shall have to return to this question. First, however, it is necessary to look rather more closely at what is meant, or what might properly be meant, by congestion in urban areas. What most people mean is that there is a shortage of living space, recreational space and transport accommodation and, perhaps in addition, that the large concentration of industry and vehicles causes high levels of noise and air pollution. In some large cities, the shortage of living accommodation and the services that, in an advanced country, are expected to go with it, is absolute, in the sense that high proportions of the population are without any housing except shanties, or share old slum houses at densities running up to several families per room. It has been mentioned in an earlier chapter that this is particularly a disease of the developing countries, where urban building simply has not been able to keep pace with the flood of new urban population, most of it flowing in from the countryside. Even Paris and Rome have some shanty colonies, but in the richer countries generally, congestion with regard to living quarters manifests itself only to a minor extent in virtual homelessness and in what is officially recognised as overcrowding. The more settled and slower-growing major cities, where supply of dwellings is more nearly in equilibrium with demand, have accommodation for almost everybody, but its price is high – in London, for instance, not far from twice that ruling in much of the rest of England.

This dearness of housing, and other characteristics which go with, or are thought of as aspects of, congestion, are largely explicable in terms of simple geometry. All great cities are great, to a major extent, because they perform a number of 'central' functions – providing services not only for their own populations, but for, or involving business with, people (some of them visitors) from the rest of the country or abroad. The location of this business is governed by the requirement that it should be as accessible as possible to as many people as possible. Some of these central functions are linked to each other, as with the various banking and financial institutions, stock exchanges, at least some associated legal services, and head offices of many industrial and commercial organisations that deal heavily with these services. The resulting business district has to be central for accessibility; accessibility makes the central area the preferred location for those shops that are highly specialised or for some other reason aspire to be regional or national in their clientele; also for theatres and other urban cultural amenities of regional significance and, of course, hotels for the visitors whom all these activities attract.

Consequently any city, especially a large one, has a central business district within which the advantages of location offered to the relevant kinds of offices, shops and the rest are such that they can outbid for space any other person or organisation with less pressing reasons for being centrally located and less ample means of competing. Regional and national capitals add large amounts of governmental office space to this district. In the largest cities, it is big; in London it comprises roughly the area bounded by the main-line rail termini, and well over a million workers commute into it daily.

Outside this urban core, residence (with the necessary purely local services) and manufacturing industry have traditionally competed for space. It is to be expected that sites adjoining the central business district will tend to be dearer the bigger the city, because the bigger the city the greater the premium that central services will find it worth paying to be in the middle of it. There is another aspect of this matter, also. To take over from residence a site on the edge of the central business district will mean displacing a certain number of people living there – probably very near to their work. If one regards the built-up area of the city as 'full up', then this displacement will mean that these people, or an equal number of others, will have to find new accommodation, which, on the assumption just made, will have to be in new housing at the periphery. Directly or indirectly, the necessity for more travel to work will be generated, and the price paid for the site on the edge of the central district must somehow include the capitalised cost of this. The bigger the city and the farther away the periphery is, the greater this price will be.

Real situations are, of course, much more complicated than we have supposed: it is possible to squeeze more people onto a given area by building higher (though this is more expensive than low-rise building); jobs are far from all being concentrated in the central business district; prices of accommodation vary not only with the location but also with the age of the building (which means that, since towns grow outwards, there is often a ring somewhere between the centre and the periphery where both rents and amenities are relatively low). But, in a general way, it is not hard to see why average cost of accommodation rises with the size of the aggregation. An additional reason why it does so is that big cities contain more than their share of the highly-paid: not just those who have to be paid more to live and work in a more expensive place, but those who are high in their professions. Some (mostly capital cities) also contain more than their share of those with high property incomes, who enjoy the metropolitan amenities. This competition from the well-to-do naturally puts up housing prices and rents.

The separation which market forces produce between residential and working areas makes for longer journeys to work the bigger the place. (The south-eastern region of England, which, of course, contains London, shows average daily journeys to work some 50 per cent longer than those in the rest of England.) This also adds to the cost of living; to some extent there is a choice between paying high rents to live near one's work and paying high travel costs (and spending time in travelling) from more distant, and cheaper, housing. Even on the periphery of a large urban area, however, sites for housing tend to be dear; for those who can readily afford the travel costs, sites near to the open country may be desirable, and the area within a given (absolute) distance of the edge of open country is a smaller proportion of the total built-up area the larger the latter becomes.

Providing for traffic flows is more difficult in a large than in a small urban area. Thinking again of the simplified situation in which travel to work in a central business district is the main source of traffic, and supposing that all travel is by road, one can see that as the built-up area and the central business district increase in size, the flow across the boundary of the business district will increase as the area (which we are supposing to be proportional to the population) of the city; that is to say, as the square of its radius; whereas the length of that boundary will increase only in proportion to the radius. Traffic (and the need for road space) across each mile of the boundary will increase; the proportion of the total area that has to be devoted to roads will rise, or else congestion will become so bad that it imposes its own limit on travel and on the working and growth of the urban area.

One is tempted to think of this – a consequence of urban growth – as the cause of the traffic congestion which now ranks as one of the chief sources of discomfort and annoyance, and of long travelling times, in the great cities of the world; but that would be a gross oversimplification. The great cities grew up in the last hundred years round systems of public transport, the biggest of them largely round their systems of suburban railways. The crisis of congestion, which is already several decades old, springs mostly from the substitution of the private car for travel by public transport, and the substitution of road goods transport (to and from the docks, especially, where the city in question is also a port) for transport by rail. In fact, the chief effect of congestion in the very large cities in advanced countries is to impose an automatic limit, not so much on the working and growth of their economies, as on the extent to which the shift from public to private transport takes place. Slow road-speeds and difficulties of parking make people travel by rail or bus (though the latter, like the private car, is subject to the delays of traffic congestion). Moreover, public transport has advantages in the large urban area that it lacks in the small one; how convenient it is to rely upon it depends largely upon the frequency of the service, and this, obviously, is proportional to the number of people wishing to travel. It is the availability of relatively frequent public transport services, on which they still rely very much more than smaller places, that has made it possible for the historic great cities to continue to grow without a total change in their layout, while suffering a degree of inconvenience from long journey times and crowded vehicles that has changed only slowly. Places such as Los Angeles, which have developed mostly in the last fifty years, in a society where almost every family has at least one car, and which has little public transport, are on a far looser pattern, and have problems of their own, of which air pollution (increasing with size, or rather with total motor vehicle use) is the best publicised, but the disadvantages suffered by the immobile poor may be more serious.

Some other disadvantages of the large built-up area are obvious; for instance, it will often have to bring its water from greater distance than smaller places, since it must either collect it over a wide area or seek some single large source, which is likely, on average, to be distant.

What all this amounts to is that, the gross overcrowding of cities with immigrants apart, there are some disadvantages that are inseparable from very large aggregations of population, though exactly what form they take depends on the physical shape that the townscape's history has given it. Congestion in the proper sense, apart from noise, air pollution, and the absence of immediately available open space, arises mostly from a physical plan and, in particular, a transport network not well adapted to the ways in which people would now prefer to live and travel. A new great city (if it had not become out-of-date by the time it was built) could probably be designed that would avoid much of it, but it would still almost inevitably, by virtue of large size, be expensive to live in.

ADVANTAGES OF SCALE

Why, then, if big aggregations are at best costly to live in, and at worst inconvenient in various specific ways, have they grown and prospered? The most obvious answer is that they are the places where the jobs are to be found – or the more lucrative jobs. What has already been said about the advantages of the largest urban concentrations as sites of office employment of many kinds, and of the provision of various other specialised services, points to the clearest reason for this: establishments providing these services get such advantages from their location that they can afford to pay their employees whatever is necessary to compensate

156

them for high rents, long journeys to work, or any other inconveniences that go with the place.

The evidence that manufacturing industry gets big advantages from being located in a large urban area is rather less clear, though there are some evident sources of economy in being near to at least one very large market, to many potential suppliers of a wide variety of inputs and to the providers of professional services. To some extent – one that probably varies greatly from industry to industry – manufacturers can afford to pay higher wages in big conurbations because they derive advantages from being there. Those who supply goods and services to the urban population without enjoying any particular advantages over those doing the same thing in smaller places may be compensated for the extra expense or inconvenience of big-town life by being able in turn to charge rather higher prices to their customers, who are rather better paid than those elsewhere. Just as countries with wide margins of comparative advantage in their export industries tend to show relatively high incomes and high costs of living, reckoned at the market rates of exchange, so big cities tend to be dear, but at least correspondingly affluent in money terms.

But the success of large cities is related to their advantages as places to live in, as well as to the jobs they provide. To set against the high money costs and some other inconveniences of life in them, there are attractions: the metropolitan amenities which draw visitors are there for the residents too; there are not only lucrative jobs, but a wide choice within daily travelling distance; although their representative inhabitant lives a long way from open country, he has superior public transport facilities for access either to the surrounding country or to anywhere in the world; along with the movement and excitement of big-town life, there is the possibility of anonymity, which appeals particularly to many young people brought up in relatively small, closed societies. All this draws in a stream of immigrants (even in mature, settled countries) and holds a proportion of metropolis-lovers, for whom London, or New York, or Paris is the only thinkable domicile – except, perhaps, Paris, or New York, or London.

OPTIMAL URBAN SIZE

Some reference has been made in an earlier chapter of this book to the theoretical possibilities of an optimal size of aggregation, and of a tendency for that size to be exceeded, which can be argued from these general considerations. In principle, there will be an optimal size for an urban aggregation if the disadvantages attached to size increase at an increasing rate as size increases, in relation to the rate at which the size-connected advantages increase. If this is so, the advantages of an increase in population will exceed the disadvantages up to a point, so that there is a net gain in average real standard of life. Then there will come a point at which the advantages of further growth are balanced by the disadvantages; then the disadvantages will predominate, and standard of life will fall with increasing population. It is hard to quantify these advantages and disadvantages, but the hypothesis just stated is, at least, a plausible one. The advantages for both productivity and the provision of the services associated with life in advanced countries increase very steeply as one moves up from very scattered populations to those mostly concentrated in small towns; it does not seem possible that the same rate of increase of advantage is maintained in moving up to bigger communities when the communities one has are already of, say, a million inhabitants each. As for the disadvantages, it seems much more likely that they will grow not much less than in proportion to size, even if they do not grow faster.

Supposing that there is an optimal size for an aggregation, what conclusions can we draw about what is likely to happen? It will suffice to mention two. First, let us take the case of the single big aggregation in a country where all the rest, the great majority, of the population are scattered in small settlements. If the aggregation were of optimal size, the net attractions (of earnings and conditions of life, taken together) which it would present in comparison with the rest of the country would be very substantial. But just for that reason, it would continue to grow. It would grow not only beyond the size that gave its residents the highest possible standard of living, but also beyond that at which the net advantage enjoyed by an additional immigrant was just offset by the extra inconvenience his arrival caused to those already there. (This is the size to which one would wish the aggregation to grow in the best interests of the country as a whole – town and country together.) It would, in fact, continue to grow until the net advantage to the average inhabitant of it in comparison with life elsewhere was zero. There would then be a strong case to be made for the proposition that the urban area was 'congested' in the sense that persuading some people to go back to the rural districts would be in the interests of the community as a whole. To the extent that the migrants would suffer in going back, it would pay the remaining inhabitants of the town to compensate them. This simple example may not be too far-fetched in relation to many developing countries, or even, though as a gross oversimplification, in relation to Paris and the rest of France.

The second deduction one can make refers to more urbanised countries in which there are a number of aggregations. The question is, will they be in stable equilibrium if they are each of optimal size? It is easy to see that the general answer is 'No'. If, for some reason which need not be specified, any considerable number of people leave one of the aggregations and distribute themselves among the others, the aggregation they have left will be removed to an appreciable extent from its former optimal situation, and its desirability as a place of work and residence will be appreciably reduced. The aggregations that gain population, on the other hand, because we are assuming that each gains only a few people, will not be pushed far above their optimal size, and their desirability will be little reduced. The tendency will, therefore, be for more and more people to follow the original migration, until the declining aggregation disappears altogether, leaving the others considerably above optimal size. Processes of this kind are likely to continue until perhaps as few as two aggregations of the kind in question are left, and these may be much beyond optimal magnitude. Two conurbations of optimal size may be in neutral equilibrium with each other provided that a transfer of people from one to the other depresses the standard of living in both by equal amounts.

There are some qualifications to this argument, arising from the probability that different aggregations have different economic functions, and different optimal sizes, and are not all in competition with each other in producing goods and services for sale outside; but in spite of this, the general principle holds that a system of aggregations will be stable only if all of them are above their optimal size. It is only then that a movement of population from one to another (or to all the others) will make the losing aggregation more attractive and the gaining ones less so, thus tending to check or reverse itself.

There is a third set of considerations that produces a probability of aggregations growing to more than optimal size; it arises simply from the fact that population is imperfectly mobile and natural

159

increase often positive. Urban communities grow not only by immigration but by natural increase of the populations already within them. If there is some optimal size for an aggregation, natural increase will eventually push the population above it, and the less sensitively net migration responds to the relative attractiveness of different environments, the more the urban community is likely to overshoot the mark.

These very broad theoretical considerations seem to suggest that there is, indeed, a considerable probability that urban aggregations may grow 'too big', so that diverting growth away from them may become a legitimate object of policy. We shall have to come back presently to the question whether there is empirical evidence that this excessive growth has actually happened, or is common; but first there is another point to which we have already referred. Even if it can be proved that, say, London or Paris is too big, that is not the same as proving that the south-east region of England, or the Paris basin is too populous, and that growth ought to be diverted away from them. The immediate moral may be that part of the populations, or what would otherwise be increments to the populations, of these great cities ought to be dispersed in satellite towns within their respective regions – not sent somewhere else altogether.

OPTIMAL REGIONAL POPULATION

If this *is* the moral, then the most obvious argument for regarding the whole metropolitan region as 'congested' and diverting growth away from it is that political or other factors prohibit the satellite town solution – that if people and industry are allowed to flow into, or to increase in, the metropolitan region they will, in practice, simply add to the sprawl and congestion of the great city. This may be so; only examination of particular cases will decide.

The second argument that might be adduced is rather more subtle; it is that even planned satellite towns within a metropolitan region (which in most cases will mean within sixty or seventy miles of the metropolis) are difficult to make reasonably independent; by virtue of the metropolitan aggregation's superior size and specialised facilities, they will generate a large volume of traffic with it, which will increase its congestion – not so badly as unplanned growth would, but still to an undesirable extent. Growth that will avoid this, the argument runs, will have to be

around rival centres so major and distant that they are outside
the metropolitan region according to any usual definition of what
a region is. This is the argument behind the French government's
designation of *métropoles d'équilibre* – existing major centres
(such as Lyons and Marseilles), all distant from Paris, as candi-
dates for deliberate development into aggregations of something
like metropolitan quality. In a different way, too, it is reflected
in much thinking about planning in the south-east region of
England. There, although it was growth within (or close to) the
region that was under discussion, it was recognised that what
might be required were a number of major 'counter-magnets' on
the edge of the region (or slightly outside it) built up into substantial places of populations running up to close on a million,
and linked to London by 'corridors of growth' with transport
(including public transport) facilities adequate to take substantial movement, including appreciable two-way commuting, without undue addition to congestion. This recognition of the careful
and massive planning necessary to develop what is essentially
the London region without increasing congestion may be regarded
as illustrating the sense in which a region may be regarded as
'congested' even when two-thirds of it consists of open country;
as compared with other regions not dominated by so enormous a
metropolitan centre, the options for growth without further congestion within it are severely circumscribed, though given wide
powers and great care they may be thought still to exist.

CONCERN AT URBAN CONCENTRATION

We have seen, then, that the concept of congestion, and still more
of a congested region (apart from the obvious and important
cases of places where an influx of people has overburdened virtually all the existing facilities) is somewhat elusive, but still mean-
ingful. What is the evidence that congestion in this rather more
subtle, long-term sense actually exists? Are the regions containing any great agglomerations 'congested' in any sense other than
that the housing and public services have not been able to catch
up with the growth of population needing them?

It is certain, at least, that there has recently been, in a number
of advanced countries, a widespread misgiving about the continued growth of the largest cities. Such misgivings are not new;
in the case of London they can be traced back for four centuries.
A hundred years ago, it was not only William Morris who

wanted to 'forget the spreading of the hideous town'. The modern phase of concern can be dated at least from the Barlow Report of 1940; but its findings illustrate the complexity of the subject. Various disadvantages of British urban life were identified, culminating in (or indicated by) adverse health conditions. But it had to be admitted that in this respect London stood well among the large British towns, and the objections to the further spread of London were based in part on its effect in depriving other parts of the country of growth, and in part on defence considerations. The more recent attitudes of planners are well represented by words in the first report of the South East Economic Planning Council (*A Strategy for the South East*):

'Our plans for the future must enable London to work as efficiently as possible. To this end the growth of London must be contained. Firm controls must be exercised to relieve traffic congestion, to reduce the difficulties and excessive costs of business firms and to make life as pleasant as possible for the individual Londoner. . . . We fully endorse the concept of holding the resident population of Greater London at or under 8 million.'

This is a view in which traffic congestion, long journeys to work and high site rents occupy perhaps the most prominent places.

Concern about the growth of Paris is also of considerable standing, but was brought to a climax by the publication in 1947 of J. F. Gravier's book, *Paris et le Désert Français*. As this title suggests, its emphasis was not so much on the positive evils of the large city as on the near monopoly which Paris possessed of both economic growth (two-thirds of the whole population growth of the country between 1861 and 1936) and of French cultural life. It was an emphasis in large part like that of the Barlow Report, considering the difference between the two cases – Britain concerned at the continued depression in other established urban centres of considerable size and standing, in comparison with the growth of London; France concerned at the relative absence of urban growth points outside Paris in a country then (and to a considerable extent still) much less urbanised as a whole than Britain. Later, attention came to be paid to the relatively high costs of development in Paris; the Third Plan (published in 1959) contained an estimate that the cost of providing housing and other services for a family in Paris was some 50 per cent higher than in the provinces, and the Fifth Plan (1966–70) put some emphasis on the more realistic pricing of services – public transport, car parking, water supply and sewerage – the real costs of which in Paris were estimated to be higher than elsewhere.

Concern in the United States about large-city problems is of more recent growth; it grew dramatically in the later sixties, when the problems in question became more acute than those of any other advanced country. The particular severity of these problems in the United States springs from a number of causes. One is that urbanisation has been rapid. Since 1940, nearly half the counties of the United States – nearly all of them rural counties – have been declining in population for, at any rate, most of the time. Pickard identifies ten 'urban regions' with populations of over a million each in 1940, growing to sixteen in 1960 – the total population of these regions growing from 54 to 101 million in the twenty years; that is to say, by 1960, nearly 60 per cent of the population lived in such regions, defined as 'coterminous areas within which urban population predominates'. This rapid rate of urbanisation owes much, of course, to the rapid increase of the United States population since the war.

A second cause is the high mobility of Americans, both in the sense that they move house frequently, and in the sense that they have high rates of private car ownership and are willing to commute over long distances. These two aspects of mobility, jointly, are presumably responsible in part, at least, for the enormous movement into residential suburbs, extending a long way out from the cities. This process has, of course, been going on for a long time in (or around) virtually all big towns, but the recent American movement has been on a vast scale and has involved much wider 'suburban' areas than ever before. By 1969, about 130 million of the 200 million inhabitants of the United States lived in 'metropolitan areas' as defined for statistical purposes (broadly, built-up areas of more than a quarter of a million population) and of these, some 72 million lived in what are broadly defined as the 'Metro rings' against 58 million in the central cities. At the same time, some three-quarters of employment growth in urban areas has been in the suburban rings (a point to which we shall return later), and the central cities have come to be inhabited largely by poor families, many of them recent arrivals, who find themselves with insufficient employment in their immediate neighbourhoods, and inadequate transport facilities to the opportunities farther afield. A third, closely connected cause is that a high proportion of the immigrants into the

163

central cities are black; their employment opportunities are diminished both through generally inferior education and through racial prejudice, so that the social problem of urban depressed areas becomes a racial problem, too. The fourth main cause of trouble is financial; the flight of population and employment from the central cities often takes them outside the administrative jurisdictions on which responsibility for those cities' problems immediately falls. If the city administrations seek to restore their revenues by higher taxation, they only accelerate the outward flight of the more well-to-do and mobile taxpayers, already hastened by the deteriorating services and environment.

None of these elements in the problem of the large United States city is either new or peculiar to that country; something of the sort has happened with cities in many countries for a very long time. The American case of the disease is, however, particularly severe by virtue mainly of the rapidity and scale of the changes involved, and to some extent of the geographical fragmentation of governmental power. Its relevance to our present subject lies in the widespread belief, nourished by urban riots and the manifest social distress in the inner cities from about 1965 onwards, that the large aggregation had become well-nigh unworkable. To divert growth to smaller communities suddenly became a widely proclaimed object of policy. Given the difficulty in American conditions of solving, by physical planning of housing and workplace location, and by reform of urban public finance, the severe sub-regional problems that have arisen within urban areas, this hostility to the large agglomeration as such, is not only understandable but to a large extent justifiable. On the other hand, while statements have been made in the United States about the rising levels of service costs with urban size, not very much convincing evidence has yet been produced there of the extent to which, and the mechanisms by which, size *necessarily* carries penalties; though presumably the considerations that have been adduced elsewhere apply in the United States as well. What has emerged is a good deal of evidence, some of it from opinion polls, of increasing dislike of big-city life – not very surprisingly in view of the problems which have just been referred to. Whatever it may be possible to do to improve the large cities in the longer run, it seems that, for the time being, a self-reinforcing mechanism is at work by which mobile taxpayers and employers flee from the central city problems, and their flight makes those problems worse.

A very different story emerges in the Netherlands. To a large extent the difference is a matter of scale; the whole country is the size only of one of the smaller American states. It is, moreover, very densely populated and has a highly centralised government. The regional problem as it emerged after the Second World War was at first mainly a matter of the decline of agricultural employment in the north and east; but concern at the growth of the great urban agglomeration often referred to as the 'Randstad'* – the horseshoe-shaped conurbation running from The Hague through Rotterdam and Utrecht to Amsterdam – eventually became apparently as important as the desire to increase the prosperity of the declining regions for their own sake. Perhaps understandably in a country where space is at such a premium, it seems to have been, literally, 'the spreading of the hideous town' that has been the main focus of attention; the fear that the carefully reserved green strips between the constituent cities of the Randstad, and the green centre within the rim, would be encroached on and lost. Concern about air and water pollution was linked with this. Alarm at the cost of large-city services and the effect of high urban rents (especially on those activities that have no reasonable alternative to a site in the congested area) have played some part, but the most powerful motive for the planning and taxation measures taken to check the Randstad's growth seems to have been a physical planner's rather than an economist's motive – to preserve the intimate mixture of urban and rural environment that the Dutch have developed and which they prize.

This very rapid glance at the nature of concern about congestion in four countries suggests that it does not spring primarily from an economic calculation of congestion costs, either within a large city, or, *a fortiori*, within a region which is likely to be far from entirely built-up. To a large extent in some countries – France most notably, but the United Kingdom also – the primary concern has been, not so much about the congested region itself, as about the outlying communities at the expense of which it was growing, and there was about the cry of congestion, initially at least, something of the air of a rationalisation. The American relatively recent but deep alarm about the large cities has been perhaps more sociological than economic. The Dutch concern seems to have been relatively simple and straightforward

*Literally, 'Rim-city'.

– broadly environmental. One could quote other cases, with their own peculiarities: the Italian concern at the excessive growth of the northern industrial cities, for instance, like the American concern, includes an element of alarm at the hostility of the established populations to the newcomers.

These various grounds for concern are all valid, as is the concern most notably in developing countries about the sheer overcrowding of urban facilities by growing, largely immigrant, populations. The point just put forward is that they are not really concerns about the inevitable and irremovable consequences of a population distribution that places very large numbers of people in particular regions; they are largely concerns about growing pains, and about the maldistribution of people and the inadequacy of provision for them within the region in question.

But in the end this is rather a pedantic distinction. The long run in which the great cities can be reshaped to serve their proper purpose, given both enormously extended populations in the regions of which they have been the historic centres, and the desire of those populations to be as mobile as modern transport allows, is, indeed, the long run in which we are all dead. Population pressure does not wait for it. Even if cities were perfectly malleable, there would still be net costs of aggregation beyond some size of the urban (and suburban) aggregate, though it is very unclear what that critical size is. Given that they are not highly malleable, that we have to live for decades with much of the urban fabric and pattern that we have now, the growing pains have to be taken as good grounds for policy. It is not even as if we knew that, in the long run, economies of scale ensure some reward for a very high degree of geographical concentration. As was pointed out in the earlier chapters of this book, the technological conditions of the fairly remote future, on which such an expectation would have to be based, are particularly obscure.

THE AUTOMATIC BRAKE ON CONGESTION

Meanwhile, it is clear that the growth of the great cities and their environs in the advanced countries has slowed down; the migration into them has in many cases reversed. To some extent this is certainly the result of policy measures. In the United Kingdom, the Greater London Council area has been falling in population for a long time, but twice as fast in the sixties as in the fifties and faster still in the early seventies. The whole south-east region's growth, about a million a decade, slowed down only slightly between the two decades as a whole (in which interval, however, national growth increased), but in 1971–3 the annual rate was reduced to a seventh of what it had previously been – a much faster deceleration than that of the UK population as a whole. Regional policy's part in diverting growth from the south-east to assisted areas, and the Greater London Council's policy of slum clearance and overspill, may be held responsible for part of this, for by no means all. The biggest visible change in population movements has been the increased flow from the south-east into the neighbouring regions, East Anglia, the south-west and, to a smaller extent the east Midlands. The area of growth surrounding London has simply become wider.

Similarly, policy measures must be held responsible for a good deal of the restraint in the growth of the Paris region. From the middle fifties onwards, manufacturing employment there ceased to grow, and its growth elsewhere was accelerated. That the incentives given for industrial growth in the outlying regions cannot claim credit for all (or even most) of this, however, is shown by the fact that the largest share of new manufacturing employment outside Paris went to the regions bordering the Paris region, even though no incentives applied there. The control of industrial building in Paris undoubtedly had an important effect, but a tendency, too, for growth to shift outwards might well have occurred even without these controls, as it did in other countries where policy was not active. In the late sixties and early seventies, the proportion of total employment growth that was in Paris rose sharply again, with the office boom; in 1971, more than half the office accommodation authorised in France was in Paris. But net migration into the Paris region halved between the 1954–62 and the 1962–8 intercensal periods, and in the latter of those periods one other region (Provence-Côte d'Azur) even had a larger absolute gain (three times as large a percentage gain) from migration than Paris had. From the beginning of the sixties, it was becoming clear that Paris was no longer thought of as overwhelmingly the most attractive magnet, and among its residents discontent with congestion and other urban disadvantages was growing. Some part of the slowing down of its growth was self-generated. The story is in some ways very similar in the Netherlands, where the substantial net migration into the three Randstad provinces began to decline sharply in the mid-fifties, and after 1960 turned into a net outward migration, of sharply increasing trend. But how far factors other than policy measures were responsible for this is obscure.

The test case, in this respect, is the United States, where there has been no effective policy directed against the growth of the large cities. There, from the sixties, it was becoming clear that the old, large urban agglomerations (even taking the relatively comprehensive delimitations given by the standard metropolitan statistical areas) were growing at less than the national average rate. This was true of Boston, New York and Chicago, among others. The large urban areas of rapid growth were the newer ones, in California, Texas, Georgia and Florida. The north-east and north-central groups of states as a whole, and the states of New York, Ohio and Illinois within them, showed substantial net outward migration. These tendencies seemed to have speeded up in the early seventies. In the country as a whole, non-metropolitan areas (that is to say, rural areas and towns of up to 50,000 that are not regarded by the statisticians as suburbs of larger centres) were growing in population faster than the metropolitan areas; this might be thought to be simply a result of the accretions at the edges of the metropolitan areas running ahead of the extension of their statistical boundaries (as, in part, it no doubt is), but for the net migration out of the whole blocks of states in which the old, large urban agglomerations lie. In that continent of high long-distance mobility, some of the movement out of the old agglomerations is long-distance movement. Moreover, some of the remote areas, long falling in population, are beginning to fill up again. In short, without any statutory curbs on urban growth, a combination of changes in technology and tastes with the congestion and social upheaval generated within the cities themselves seems to be promoting a massive population dispersion, such as policy makers in other countries have sought to bring about.

The question that naturally arises, therefore – since so many changes seem to come to Europe from the west – is whether the regional policies of the European countries we have considered, insofar as they were concerned to check metropolitan growth, were really necessary. Towards an answer, it may be appropriate to offer one final consideration, drawn from the theoretical discussion of optimal aggregation sizes earlier in this chapter. If there is an optimal size for an aggregation, we saw that population would eventually grow beyond it, and the standard of life would deteriorate in relation to that elsewhere until, through net outward migration, the growth became self-limiting. But when that point is reached, the social optimal size, at which the benefit to a migrant in going from country to town just equals the extra congestion-damage he inflicts on the townspeople, is long past. Wherever people move voluntarily, but where their movement has adverse effects on the lives of others of which the movers cannot take account, the automatic check on movement comes too late. The sad deterioration of American large-city life in the late sixties and early seventies gives this apparently abstract principle all too much relevance and realism.

CHAPTER 8

Regional Policy

Regional problems may, for the most part, be classified very simply into those arising from the fact that the increase of work and that of people wanting it are not in the same place, and those arising because, although the work and the workers are in the same place, it is for some reason the wrong place. The first of these families of problems challenges policy makers to decide whether it is better to try to move the work, or the workers, or, to some extent, both; and then to devise ways of doing it. The second requires them to decide what is the right place (or more realistically, what is the right spatial pattern of distribution) for population and economic activity, and, again, to devise ways of distributing them according to it. The extent to which policy makers feel themselves challenged, or obliged, to attempt these tasks, and the political constraints within which they have to operate in performing them, vary greatly from one country to another.

CONTROL OF LARGE AGGREGATIONS

The variation in the influence of political and philosophical climate is perhaps most dramatically exemplified in connection with the second family of problems – particularly the aspect of it to which we gave some attention in the last chapter: namely, the problems of urban communities that grow, or threaten to grow, too big, according to ideas widely held at the time in question. There are, of course, great difficulties in deciding where excessive size begins; it is a matter on which opinions vary greatly from time to time, as well as from country to country. But, granted that there is a widespread feeling that some urban aggregation (or perhaps more than one) is too big, what it is proposed to do about it, and what gets done show an enormous range of variation. We have already referred, in the last chapter, to the great difference in this respect between the United States on the one hand and the Netherlands (and we might have added the United Kingdom and France) on the other.

City-planning regulations date, in the United States, as in the United Kingdom, mainly from the early years of the present century, and they often include elaborate 'zoning' laws, prescribing both the kinds of activity and certain characteristics of the buildings for specified areas; but they vary widely from state to state and city to city. Their main deficiency, however, in relation to control of urban growth, is that the larger urban areas consist of a great many separate jurisdictions – the average Standard Metropolitan Statistical Area contains 90 – so that the kind of large-scale (almost regional) land-use planning that is necessary for surrounding such a large urban area with a 'green belt' is lacking. The North American devotion to the grassroots democracy of the local community presents difficulties when many local communities have merged into a sprawling built-up area, the constituent parts of which are highly interdependent. Moreover the difficulty of getting positive action, for development or redevelopment, on a metropolitan scale is increased by that of securing the money for it, since the small jurisdictions tend to be financially independent. It is important to remember that, despite its historic great cities, the United States was until relatively recently essentially a country of free-standing small towns. It was also (and, relatively speaking, still is) a country with plenty of space.

The contrast between this state of affairs and that in the Netherlands has already been referred to. The Dutch have long been aware of land as a scarce resource – if only from their knowledge of the cost of reclaiming more of it from the sea. While their provinces exercise some administrative functions, moreover, the reality of political power, especially the power of taxation, is highly centralised. These are just the conditions one would expect to promote a national policy of land-use planning.

Again, British conditions stand in some sort of contrast to those of the United States. The great urbanisation of the country happened much earlier – it was going fastest a hundred years ago, and was largely complete by the nineties, when the system of local government was comprehensively reformed and given the shape which it retained until recently, with (by American standards) a relatively small number of local authorities at the level at which, subsequently, planning came to be done. More and more, also, the central government became the paymaster and the supervisor of local authorities.

171

In France, to take another important contrasting case, there has been one of the most strongly centralised governments in the world, ever since Napoleon, (indeed, even longer). The simple contrast 'Paris and the French desert' describes not only the concentration of development which became the dominant cause for concern among planners after the war, but also the concentration of political power which made it relatively easy to do something about it.

These differences resulted in different degrees and kinds of action against excessive concentration of population and industry. In the United States, although there was much alarm at the end of the sixties and in the early seventies, in fact no measures of national policy resulted, and by the mid-seventies national pronouncements indicative of intentions to take action seemed to have ceased – perhaps because the spontaneous movements towards decentralisation, referred to in the last chapter, seemed to be removing at least some of the grounds for concern. The financial difficulties of many city administrations, due mainly to their having been left with the social problems but without the taxpayers, remain, as witness the disastrous situation of New York City in 1975.

In the Netherlands, concern at the excessive growth of the Randstad came into prominence only gradually; it at first held second place to concern at unemployment in the rural areas of the east and north, part of the policy remedy for which, in the earlier postwar years, was the subsidisation of emigration to the Randstad – taking the workers to the work. In the late fifties, part of the policy was reversed, while subsidisation of the movement of industry out of the Randstad and neighbouring areas was retained. Whether as a result of this or for other reasons, the net migration of about 10,000 a year into the Randstad provinces, which had continued from the end of the war until the mid-fifties, was actually reversed by 1965.

Subsequently, in 1971, under pressure of further development (including the great office boom, which spread through all the metropolitan cities of the advanced countries in the sixties) proposals were made for heavy taxation of industrial and commercial building in the Randstad. After long controversy, however, this was abandoned (except for Rotterdam) in favour of direct control by licensing, which is to apply to the whole of the congested area. Meanwhile, a movement of some 8,000 civil service jobs out of the Randstad had been approved, to take place between

172

1974 and 1978. This record shows, at all events, a fairly prompt response of policy to the perception of a problem, and some *prima facie* evidence that at least the earlier policy measures had some effect, though to this matter of their effectiveness we shall have to return.

THE CASE OF LONDON

In both the United Kingdom and France, as we have already noted, concern of some sort at the growth of the capital city and its region goes back a long way; in the case of London, to trace it no further back, the beginnings of a plan for Greater London were being formulated before the Second World War. At the same time the Barlow Report was being written, with its recommendations both that the growth of London would be checked and that decentralisation from congested urban areas in general should be promoted, by means including the building of satellite towns. At the end of the war came a series of measures in the spirit of this. The New Towns Act of 1946 established the machinery for state development of new towns through corporations set up for that purpose. The Town and Country Planning Act of 1947 established planning control over land use throughout the country with central monitoring of the plans which local planning authorities were required to draw up, and central licensing of all substantial new building for manufacturing purposes. The Abercrombie Plan for Greater London demanded both the restriction of further extension of the built-up area by a 'green belt' within which building not connected with rural activities would be prohibited, and the absorption outside the belt, partly at least in new satellite towns, of overspill both from slum clearance (insofar as it reduced the density of population) and from population growth.

All this established both a physical master plan and the legislative means of controlling the growth of a great city such as did not exist elsewhere. To a substantial extent it may be judged to have resulted in successful action. The green belt was established. The resident population enclosed within it declined (by nearly a million between 1951 and 1973). Manufacturing employment within it also fell. Nine new towns were established, and arrangements for receiving overspill population from London were made with more than twenty other towns in (or bordering on) the south-east.

Three things may be said to have gone differently from what was envisaged in the plan, however. The first was that the national population began to grow quite rapidly after 1955, whereas the London Plan had been drawn up against the background of the slow growth – and threat of actual decline – in the thirties. Even the Royal Commission on Population, which reported in 1949, expected only a slow growth in the next thirty years. The result was, in the first place, a greater natural increase than had been expected within London itself. This reached its peak in the early sixties. These circumstances, however, as we have noted, did not prevent a fall in the resident population of Greater London itself. What they did assist in producing was a very rapid rise in the population of the zone beyond the green belt – the Outer Metropolitan Area, in which the London new towns were situated.

A related factor, the second of the unforseen circumstances just referred to, was the great attractive power of these new towns, and in a rather smaller degree, of other sites in the Outer Metropolitan Area and the zone still farther out, the Outer South-East. In the fifties they drew in not only industry displaced from London, but industrial expansion from the rest of the country. So far as population and manufacturing industry were concerned, therefore, the old worry that London was attracting more than its share was assuaged, but a similar worry took its place, relating to the whole south-east region. In the sixties, the strengthening of regional policy – the combination of control on industrial building with incentives to establish in the more peripheral parts of the country – eased this worry, too. At a time when industrial building plans approved in the country as a whole were following an upward trend, those approved in the south-east fell.

The third unforseen factor, probably the most important of all, was the enormous boom in office work and office building, which began in the fifties, but accelerated in the sixties. Like the other metropolitan cities of the advanced countries at this time, London proved to have a far greater attraction as a site for offices than ever it had had for manufacturing industry. The consequence of this was that total employment in London increased, despite the fall in both resident population and manufacturing employment, and that the volume of daily travel to work from outside it grew. Action to deal with this situation began to be taken from 1963, when the Location of Offices Bureau was set up to promote and assist the decentralisation of office activities. In 1964, a control by licence of office building in London (and also in Birmingham) was instituted – in addition, of course, to the normal town planning controls. How effective these measures were it is hard to say, especially as there was a great deal of building for which planning permission was already granted when the control was instituted, and applications for such permission had already passed their peak.

There was, however, a great deal of office decentralisation in the sixties. So far as the private sector was concerned, it was largely to sites within Greater London, but away from the old central business district; then to sites farther afield, urban islands that had been isolated in the green belt, and towns outside that belt, up to sixty or a hundred miles from London. The publicity and persuasion of the Location of Offices Bureau must have made a contribution here; on the face of it, however, it would seem that the great rise in London rents was the immediate motive force in many cases. This, in turn, was partly a consequence of office building control, which made office space in London scarcer than it would otherwise have been. In addition, some 30,000 headquarters Civil Service jobs were dispersed (or scheduled for dispersal) from London in the decade following a review of the possibilities in 1963 and, of the extra Civil Service posts created, some 20,000 were set up (or to be set up) outside London. For these moves of public sector offices, the average distance was greater.

But some of the movement can probably be regarded as a continuation of the evolutionary process by which great cities select those activities for which they have the strongest comparative advantage, and squeeze out the rest. The offices squeezed out residences and factories; now those offices which regard it as most important to be in central London are squeezing out the others. In any case, improvement of transport and telecommunications reduces the importance of a central London site, at least for some office activities; for a good many it has been estimated that the ideal location, where the combination of rents, wages and communication expenses is at a minimum lies about a hundred miles out of London. It is noteworthy that the volume of daily travel into central London seems to have reached a peak in the early sixties.

In the sixties, various reviews were undertaken of the London plan, and a modification of strategy gradually gained favour. In view of the rapid growth, and prospective growth, of the south-east as a whole (despite the checks applied to it) and the increased pressure of employment, if not of residence, inside London itself, the green belt was felt to have been drawn too tight. A strategy of 'corridors of growth', stretching out from London to large 'counter-magnet' towns at the edges of the region, came into favour. After 1965, however, natural increase of population began to fall, and immigration from overseas had already been subjected to strict control, so that the prospects of population growth changed again. The story of attempts to control the growth of London so far is one of serious endeavour in a generally favourable political setting; but it illustrates clearly the hazards that beset any activity in which a view has to be taken of broad trends in the economy for decades ahead.

THE CASE OF PARIS

The corresponding story of Paris is in some important respects parallel, though with interesting differences. There, too, schemes for decentralisation had been considered even before the end of the war. Subsequently, in 1950, the Minister of Reconstruction and Housing produced a report advocating comprehensive territorial planning throughout the country, *l'aménagement du territoire*, the main end of which was to be decentralisation from Paris, cultural as well as economic. Some measures to promote decentralisation were enacted, but with little obvious effect. In 1954–5, however, more positive and comprehensive measures were taken. They included both licensing of new industrial establishments and extensions in the Paris region (an area with a population of 8 million) and various inducements (to which we shall refer later) to transfers to the provinces.

These measures were apparently effective, at least so far as factory construction was concerned. The Paris region's share of the national total came down from a third to a tenth in eight years, and by the early sixties the factory space in the region was declining. It was already becoming apparent, however, as in London, that the real comparative advantage of a capital region is in office work. In 1959, the building of large office blocks was subjected to licensing, and in the following year a tax on construction in the region was added. At the same time, in an act of policy that has had no parallel in the United Kingdom, a dozen of the large institutions of higher education were banished

176

from Paris to the provinces. Yet in the intercensal period 1954–62, the population of the Paris region had still grown twice as fast, relatively, as that of the rest of the country. The office work and service industry boom had far outweighed the decline of manufacturing. Moreover, the new growth outside the Paris region, like that outside London, was heavily concentrated in the adjoining regions, not the more distant ones.

In the next phase of regional policy, therefore, a heavy emphasis was placed upon encouragement of the so-called *métropoles d'équilibre*; not quite the same thing as the projected 'counter-magnets' of the planners in the English south-east region, which were intended to be the ends of corridors of growth, only sixty miles or so from London, but eight major urban centres, all but one (Lyons-St Etienne) on the very edges of the country, as far from Paris as possible. We shall have to consider this policy in its own right later. For the moment it is relevant to observe that, in the intercensal period 1962–8, all but one of the *métropoles d'équilibre* did, in fact, grow in population at a faster percentage rate than the Paris region, and two of them together (Lyons and Marseilles) even grew more absolutely. The exception was the largely textile centre, Lille-Roubaix Tourcoing, the particular difficulties of which we examined in an earlier chapter, though even that grew. But the ring of regions around Paris still increased its industrial employment at twice the national rate, and gained in population by net immigration, despite the decline of the local agriculture.

As for the Paris region itself, it continued to grow in population faster than the rest of the country, but its share of the national increase had fallen, in comparison with the previous intercensal period, from a third to a quarter. Its growth was largely due to the influx of overseas immigrants, without which its net gain by immigration would have been small. As it was, its total annual net gain by immigration was reduced by more than a third from that of the period 1954–62.

A COMPARISON

In comparing this situation with that of Greater London, one has to remember that the Paris region is very much the larger area (though not very different in total population); its outer ring corresponds to part of the Outer Metropolitan ring outside London, within which population has continued to grow fast, and into which there is still net immigration. With due allowance for this degree of uncertainty, one may say that the experiences of the two capital regions have been remarkably similar. In both, the first apparent result of attempts at control, and of other forces operating in the postwar period, was to push the zone of rapid growth farther away from the central city. In both, further measures apparently resulted in some diversion of growth to parts of the country far from the metropolis. In both, the internal net migration to the metropolitan region has been brought down to a low level or actually reversed. In both, the policy makers' initial concentration was on moving manufacturing industry, and the magnitude of the office boom caught them by surprise. In both, too, new satellite towns have been used (considerably earlier in the UK) to ameliorate the pattern of growth within the broad metropolitan region. Many of these elements are shared also by the history of the Dutch Randstad.

The other, rather more disturbing characteristic that all three share is the difficulty confronting any assessment of the influence that policy has in fact had, in view, especially, of the fact that the recent decentralisation of activity from them has a parallel in the United States, where there was hardly any policy at all. One must suppose, however, that the measures taken in the three European countries had some effect. They seem to have diverted growth to a substantial extent from those areas of initially rapid growth that were not congested, to more distant regions, and they must have hastened departure from the congested areas, too. In their absence, therefore, metropolitan congestion would probably have got a good deal worse before it limited itself.

So much for the most notable of the efforts to prevent the excessive accumulation of people and work in what, for reasons of congestion in these instances, were regarded as being the 'wrong' places. The complement of these efforts are those that have been directed to bringing both jobs and people in matching numbers to new sites – the development of new centres of economic activity. However, as most of these have been part of a strategy for either reducing congestion within a congested region (as with the London and Paris New Towns) or for reviving or developing regions threatened with labour surplus, we shall not look at them as a separate category of their own, but we shall return to some of them in due course.

178

MISMATCHING GROWTH OF POPULATION AND JOBS

Taking the workers to the work

We may therefore turn now to the cases where people and jobs – or, more accurately, the increases of numbers of people and of jobs – were in different places. The 'problem areas' hitherto discussed in this book (except the 'congested' areas) are, of course, all regions in which the growth of jobs has been inadequate to meet the growth of people wanting them. The first question for policy, as we have already noted, is whether to reduce this mismatch by taking the work to the workers or the workers to the work.

Taking the workers to the work has been the less commonly adopted solution. (Some might say that, when it is done, it hardly ranks as a 'regional' measure in any case, but that proposition as it stands does not bear very close examination.) It was, however, the first policy adopted in the United Kingdom for dealing with the problem of severe localised unemployment in 1928. In the decade that followed, it proved neither very successful nor very popular. It is clearly not a very good policy unless there is a shortage of labour (or, at least, of the specific kinds of labour that are moved) in the areas of destination; otherwise the incomers simply deprive residents of jobs that they would otherwise have had. There was little shortage of labour anywhere in the United Kingdom between 1928 and 1938. But, in addition, the policy was unpopular in the depressed regions from which movement was assisted, mainly because, as we noted in an earlier chapter, emigration even of the unemployed depresses regional purchasing power and thus regional service employment, unless what spending power the unemployed have is provided entirely by taxpayers in the region where they live. It was also unpopular because it was seen as diminishing the probability of the alternative solution, an inflow of industry seeking available labour – though that was not very probable in any case when labour was available everywhere.

We have noted also that assistance of migration to prosperous areas was one of the first policies adopted to deal with decline of agricultural employment in the Netherlands after the Second World War, and that this policy was abandoned (so far as it related to migration to the Randstad) for reasons which, in fact, had applied in the United Kingdom as well – namely, that the migrants were going to areas where there was deemed to be danger of congestion. The point is a very simple and general one: it is a good idea to subsidise (or otherwise assist) this movement of either labour or jobs only if the destination of the factor one is seeking to move is regarded as a desirable one in general, a desirable growth point. Congested areas are not so regarded.

The country where mobility in search of work has been given most positive assistance is Sweden. The system there is a comprehensive one, and has been maintained even where it was manifestly assisting depopulation of the northern areas which policy was also resisting. In fact, relocation of labour *within* those areas was thought to be necessary to their economic health, but no distinction in relocation allowances seems to have been made between workers who moved within the assisted area and those who moved out; it was left to other measures of policy to keep, or increase, the working population of those areas by subsidising and otherwise assisting the creation of new jobs there. In the United Kingdom there is still some provision for assisting movement of labour, but it has played a small part in comparison with measures to move jobs.

Elsewhere, in France, Italy and the United States, for instance, since the war, the main reason for not enhancing labour mobility deliberately has been simply that labour was moving from the countryside to the big cities in any case at a rate that was socially and politically embarrassing. That, however, is not to say that these movements were not even indirectly the results of policy; improved education in rural areas, in particular, is a great promoter of outward mobility of their populations, quite apart from the effects it may have (and is often designed to have) in helping to induce external enterprise to come in, or indigenous enterprise to develop.

The balance between these different effects of what Americans call 'investment in human capital' in depressed or backward regions is hard to predict, or even to assess after the event. The Appalachian Programme, which is the largest United States joint federal and state regional development scheme, started in the mid-sixties with 1·3 billion dollars of federal aid, spread over six years, and with matching state funds. The largest share of this went to road building, but for the rest the programme has concentrated heavily on education, training and health, in the full realisation (indeed partly on the ground) that population is the most mobile resource. By the early seventies some parts of the area had shown a reversal of their long-standing population decline through outward migration, but this was part of a widespread change in the pattern of American population growth in which many factors were at work. Federal assistance in other economic development regions, including New England and the Atlantic coastal area of the south, has been to a greater extent devoted to physical infrastructure.

Taking the work to the workers
In contrast to those policies that have aimed at assisting movement of workers to the places where there is already work for them, places of existing labour shortage, there stand those much more numerous policies that have aimed to do the opposite – to cause jobs to be created in the places where there is actually or potentially a surplus of labour. For this, all kinds of instruments and strategies have been employed. Employers have been seduced with subsidies on capital expenditure in the assisted regions, with subsidies on their wage bills there, with loans on favourable terms, with tax concessions, with publicly provided factory buildings at favourable rents, with housing provision for managers and key workers whom they would require to take with them, with training grants for the labour they employ, with a great variety of improvements in facilities and environment from new roads to the landscaping of spoil-heaps. They have also been threatened with, or subjected to, prohibition of their schemes for new establishments or for expansion in any areas other than those to which governments wish them to go, and occasionally, as we have seen, to special taxes in the congested areas which governments wish especially to avoid or to leave. We shall make a very general review of these instruments, without entering into the intolerable detail of a country-by-country survey – one feature common to the instruments of regional policy in practically all countries where it exists is the bewildering frequency with which they have been changed. First, however, we shall consider briefly one of the main questions of regional strategy that arises in this connection – whether inducements, or aid, should be given to industry wherever it chooses to establish itself within broad assisted areas, or whether, on the other hand, efforts should be directed to the creation of one or more growth points, perhaps with a selected industrial character.

181

GROWTH-POINT STRATEGY

The case for selecting promising growth points and confining official help to them is strongest when the help required is great, and, without some impulse from outside there is likely to be an absence of those external economies on which some kinds of industry, at all events, depend. In other words, it is strongest where the area to be assisted is an agricultural or a mining one, with a pattern of settlement and a network of transport and public utility provision unsuitable for its future development, so that these amenities have to be provided, and the first industrial or other establishments to come in will face a period of being very much on their own. The only economical way of providing the infrastructure required in these circumstances is to choose a site in the region as accessible as possible (or as cheap as possible to make accessible) from the main existing centres of economic activity in other regions, to make its communications with them adequate and, in effect, to build a town (or to enlarge a town that is there already) so that it can collect the scattered populations from the surrounding country and become a centre with a fair-sized labour market and with good services and amenities.

We have noted in an earlier chapter the extreme case for such growth centres that exists in the north of Sweden, where the authorities have estimated that, in order to provide the amenities that are likely to hold its people, a town must have a minimum population of 30,000 – a number which in that part of the world comprises the population of a very big area. In the long run, comprehensive planning with communities of viable size is envisaged, but in the meantime, in the face of rapid depopulation of the inland areas, a generous system of investment grants and transport subsidies was instituted. The problems that arose illustrate some of the difficulties of the growth-point strategy. The existing towns of viable size are mostly on the coast. The question was, should aid be confined to the inland towns, handicapped as they were, or should they be regarded as expendable, and hope be pinned on the coast towns? In fact, in the first instance, the same incentives were applied to both. Later, when most of the new jobs proved, indeed, to go to the coast towns, a preferential measure of assistance was given to the inland area. The essential difficulty is, of course, that a growth point, one with either artificial or natural advantages, will, at least up to a point, grow at the expense of less favoured places. In rescuing any declining area, therefore, the same question arises as confronts a general fighting a defensive campaign: What is defensible? What is expendable? If he concentrates his defence too much, existing communities are lost that might have been saved; if he disperses it too much, everything may be lost. In regional, as opposed to military strategy, however, there is the complication that the people concerned all have votes.

At the other end of the size-range are the large growth points regarded by the French planners as being required to hold their own in competition (though at a distance) against Paris – the *métropoles d'équilibre*. There, of course, existing large cities were chosen to give the best possible start. The assistance given to them was mostly in infrastructure investment, planning and, later an investment grant for office and similar development. They were not given special privileges with regard to manufacturing. Their growth, in the later sixties was, as we have already noted, rapid. But, having demonstrated their power to grow faster, proportionately, than Paris itself, they began to arouse apprehensions; partly because they were felt to be growing to some extent at the expense of their respective hinterlands, partly because, as they grew big, the costs of further development in them began to show as being greater than those of accommodating the same number of extra people in smaller places. A complex of over a million (like Lyons), based on an old urban core, is apt to generate quite a lot of traffic congestion, and is of the marginal size at which an underground railway network is barely justifiable. As in the United States, at the same time and after a period of comparably rapid urban growth, the virtues of small and medium-sized towns *(villes moyennes)* began to be rediscovered in the early seventies. Little overt discrimination in favour of large centres now remains. The planning process no doubt produces some discrimination between different towns implicitly, through the distribution of infrastructure investment, but the incentives and checks to private investment, though geographically complex, essentially express control of Paris (and now to some extent of Lyons), favour to the south-western half of France generally, and special favour to limited 'black spots', of which the old industrial areas of the northern frontier are the most conspicuous.

Italy illustrates the problems of a rather different kind of growth-point strategy. The original procedure after the establishment of the Cassa per il Mezzogiorno was to invite local authorities to form consortia to designate growth centres for industrial development, within which the Cassa would provide most of the necessary infrastructure. The number of responses was large; the Cassa sorted out, initially, a dozen proposed development areas with populations of 200,000 or more, and double that number of smaller 'nuclei', which were intended to develop industry mainly for local markets. (More of both were subsequently added.) It was not a very high concentration of effort, but even so, given the tendency of enterprise to make its own selection of the most accessible or otherwise favoured sites, a number of the large coastal cities – especially Naples and Bari – were regarded, by the early seventies, as seriously congested, whereas much of the interior, starved of both public and private investment, was complaining bitterly. The result, as in the very different circumstances of the Swedish Norrland, and in France, was a shift of emphasis to more widespread infrastructure investment and modification of the incentives towards greater dispersion. Very high investment incentives were provided for small projects, the highest being reserved for those in areas of heavy depopulation.

These instances may serve to show that 'growth-point' strategy, which was very fashionable in several countries in the sixties, is difficult in practice. In some countries it has played no part in policy or if it has, the number of 'growth points', 312 in Germany, for instance, has been so large that it differed little from a policy defined in terms of broad, continuous areas. The United Kingdom is one country in which it has played relatively little part, except insofar as the New Towns and government-provided industrial estates have been foci of growth. The fact seems to be that, the more a country is urbanised already, and provided with reasonably serviceable infrastructure, the less this strategy, in its original form, is called for. The policies that seem to be related to it, such as new towns, are either part of the replanning of great towns or, in closer relation to the original growth-point strategy, centres for the redevelopment of run-down mining areas.

One more developed strategy related to the original concept must be mentioned: the strategy of establishing an 'industrial complex'. The underlying idea is the very simple one that, where industrial establishments depend upon one another in such a way that they benefit by being close together, no one of them will be anxious to go to an area where the others are not already present

– so none of them will be willing to go, unless it is possible to contrive what might be called a 'conspiracy' for them all to go together. The most famous example in Europe of an attempt to bring this about is the plan, instituted in the mid-sixties, to establish a particular kind of metal-working complex at Taranto, near the large state-owned steelworks which had been allotted to that location mainly for reasons of regional development, but had itself few links with the economy of its neighbourhood. The subsequent experience of long delays illustrates the point that, when such results have to be obtained by persuading a considerable number of units (31 at Taranto) to agree to a particular scheme, the difficulty rises considerably faster than in proportion to that number. It is a strategy that is more effective where the state is itself in a strong position to step in and fill gaps in the jigsaw with public enterprise. It is also obvious that this strategy is the more necessary, or more worthwhile, the more remote the location in question is from industry of any of the relevant kinds.

Otherwise there have been few attempts to create concentrations of particular industries as a part of regional policy. France is the chief exception: government influence has been used to promote some localisation of the electronics industry in Brittany and aerospace industries near Toulouse. But localisation has been carried no further than that. The French, like the British, have been at pains to disperse the motor industry. In the United Kingdom, the early thinking on regional policy favoured diversification – not having too many of a region's eggs in one basket – and in fact, the postwar trend has been strongly towards diversification, apparently largely spontaneously, though Scotland has, partly of intent, developed a centre of the electronics industry second only to that in the London area.

THE INSTRUMENTS OF INDUSTRIAL LOCATION POLICY

Infrastructure versus cash

From this short consideration of the spatial strategy of regional development aid, let us now turn to its instruments. Perhaps it is natural to start with the provision or improvement of the regional infrastructure as a means of initiating regional development. It is obvious that, where there are serious deficiencies of infrastructure – bad communications, water supply, schools and so on – an improvement may be a necessary condition of getting new enterprise to come in, or to blossom there. It is therefore important

185

when the region to be helped is rural, or when it is an old mining area, with scattered communities and perhaps with unsightly spoil-heaps and dereliction – largely the same circumstances in which, as we have just noted, the strongest case can also be made for a growth-point strategy. It is at its least important, relatively, when the area in question is urbanised and, though suffering from decline in its industries, not too run-down; though in such cases some help with the cleaning-up of the environment (of the kind that has started, but of which there is so much more to do, in Lancashire and Yorkshire) and special help with rehabilitation of housing, may be very necessary.

The question is, how far is infrastructure provision or improvement not only necessary but also sufficient to promote development? Again, the broad answer ought to be obvious: it is sufficient if there is such pressure for industrial (or commercial) growth that employers will move into any community where labour is available, provided only that local services and amenities are not seriously below the general standard. This was the situation perhaps most notably in western Germany in, roughly, the years 1959–66, after full employment was attained, and before the combination of economic recession and the flood of immigrant workers released the pressure of search for pockets of labour not yet fully occupied. Employers spread out rapidly into the small towns and villages of the countryside, where agricultural labour was being released. It was, of course, in this period that the pressure of demand was so effective in also mopping up the labour released by coal mining, in the highly urbanised Ruhr district where remoteness and lack of infrastructure were not serious problems. The best contribution to solving the problem of a depressed region is always to engineer excess demand for labour in the country as a whole – if other considerations do not forbid it – and in these circumstances the removal even of those infrastructure deficiencies that are positively crippling will suffice to bring employers into almost any place.

But frantic search for labour is not the universal condition in countries with depressed regions and, in its absence, the presumption seems to be that to attract enterprise by superior infrastructure alone is expensive; it would be more economical to the government, and much more economical to the community in real terms, to use some of the infrastructure expenditure to provide cash inducements, instead. This seems to be one lesson of Dutch experience with the infrastructure (and industrial training) expenditure at the refurbished and expanded town of Emmen in the early fifties: it was found necessary to provide building grants to attract industry. Italy, where infrastructure improvement has clearly been very important, in that most southern locations would have had very little chance of attracting industry without it, has gradually increased its inducements, in, the form mostly of cheap loans, capital grants and tax remissions. France, in the sixties, not only concentrated infrastructure expenditure in the depressed west of the country on growth centres to a very considerable extent, but also paid higher investment grants in these centres than outside them; the grants were regarded as necessary to ensure the full use of the infrastructure, rather than the infrastructure being considered an attraction that would enable grants to be reduced or dispensed with. In Britain, the New Towns proved to be highly attractive to industry in the London area (a zone favoured by industry in any case) but in Scotland and the north-east they have, in general, needed all the inducements that applied in those areas to attain their moderate level of success.

Improvement of infrastructure has, in the past, been the most favoured measure of regional policy in the United States, and has been favoured in some other countries by those who wish to see overt government intervention in the conduct of private industry limited; but its own limitations when used alone are suggested by what has just been said. Improvement in the quality of labour, through vocational education and training, is in some ways a similar measure of aid and, as has been noted earlier, it has come into favour in the United States, and especially in the Appalachian Programme. The case for it is clearly strongest where the area in question has training and educational facilities below the national average, or (what may not be quite the same thing) has an unusually large proportion of its resident population in need of education, training or retraining. In a centralised state that aims in the ordinary course of events to distribute educational and training services among its regions in accordance with need, little in the way of special aid programmes will be called for in this connection; in one where the services in question are locally provided and locally financed to any large degree, the opposite will be the case. Vocational training and retraining are obviously of great importance in any modern, or modernising, society; Sweden probably sets the highest example in the world. It has to be faced, as we have already noted in connection with Swedish and American experience, that such training tends to increase geographical mobility of labour, even when not accompanied, as it is most notably in Sweden, by grants specifically to assist geographical movement, and the net result of such measures, applied either generally or specifically to a depressed region, may well be that, if nothing else is done, the exodus of labour will be promoted more than the introduction of jobs. If this is not acceptable, it is obviously better to counter it by other measures to bring in enterprises, or to encourage their growth locally, than it is to fall short in giving people the help they need for adapting their talents to economic opportunities. The difficulty, in practice, is often to decide for which kinds of opportunity people in a given situation can best be prepared; none of the practical arts has a worse record of failure than manpower planning.

Cash inducements: capital versus labour subsidies

This brings us to the subsidies and other cash inducements that have been used to create jobs in areas where they are needed. Most countries have used such measures. By far the commonest are those that help with investment in the assisted areas: either loans at less than the rate of interest at which the beneficiary could borrow commercially, or grants towards the cost of machinery or buildings, or concessions in regard to the rate at which capital may be depreciated for tax purposes – a higher rate of depreciation benefits the taxpayer by postponing his payment, and thus raises the present value of his prospective income net of tax. Both cheap loans and grants in aid of capital expenditure may be presumed to confer a benefit related closely to the amount of the investment. Free or accelerated depreciation of capital, which was the most important single British inducement for a few years in the sixties, is related to capital outlay – indeed, is of benefit at all – only insofar as the enterprise in question does, in fact, make profits, and thus become subject to tax on them. Many new enterprises starting in assisted areas do not make any, or much, profit for a number of years; so the benefit of accelerated depreciation to them is small or non-existent. Advocates of this instrument say that it is good in that it benefits the efficient more than the inefficient; opponents of it say that it arbitrarily benefits the multi-plant firm that is making profits on its established undertakings (though not yet in its new plant in the assisted area) in comparison with the single-plant firm that is starting business in the assisted area, and that, in any case, it is before they have begun to make profits that even the subsequently efficient may need help. They also point out that many business-men are not sufficiently sophisticated in their profit calculations to understand that accelerated depreciation benefits them at all.

But against all inducements related to the amount of invest-ment, insofar as they are not matched by others related to the wage bill, it is possible to bring the charge that they operate more powerfully on capital-intensive industries and thus tend to shift such industries, preferentially, into the assisted areas. This, on the face of it, is an odd way to assist regions whose chief trouble is a surplus of labour. Indeed, a highly capital-intensive plant, employing few people, may do the region in which it is located very little good. The benefits from it go mainly to its proprietors and, one hopes, to the buyers of its output, both of which groups of people are likely to live mostly outside the region. Statistical evidence has been produced to suggest that this selection of capital-intensive industry for the assisted regions happened, at one stage at least, in the United Kingdom. It would be surprising if it had not happened elsewhere, too. Some apprarent cases in point, however, for example the heavy industries established in the south of Italy, are there mainly because they were in public or semi-public ownership, and thus could be located directly in such a way as to suit regional policy.

Inducements related to employment, or the wage bill, have been rarer, though insofar as the immediate object of regional policy is often to promote employment in the assisted area, one might have expected subsidies on employment to play a prominent part. The United Kingdom Regional Employment Premium is the main example, and even it has never succeeded in subsidising the wage bill to more than about half the extent to which investment was subsidised. Its mode of operation is, of course, rather dif-ferent from that of investment grants and the like: it confers an immediate benefit on all enterprise of the assisted kinds in the relevant areas in proportion to their employment; they do not have to wait for its help until they are next increasing their plant. Its effect on new investment is presumably indirect, through the increased funds made available to enterprises in the assisted areas, or the increased prospect of profit it creates for them, or both. It was intended by its originators as a device for improving the competitive power of the assisted regions, equivalent to a devalu-ation of their currencies. Like any cash assistance to regions, how-ever, it has an additional effect in simply stimulating their economies by the increase of regional demand. It is perhaps not surprising that, while a measurable effect on employment in the assisted regions has been attributed to it by various investigations, any effect on industrial investment is much more elusive.

Negative controls
Apart from inducements, the main means of getting enterprises to go where they are wanted is to control their ability to go (or expand) anywhere else. In this kind of control, the United Kingdom is the pioneer, with its system of Industrial Development Certificates dating from the Town and Country Planning Act of 1947. There can be very little doubt that it has been important in securing whatever results British regional policy has achieved, though its contribution is hard to separate from those of other instruments; until recent years, it has generally been administered with a degree of rigour related to the urgency of regional issues, to which the power of the current inducements was also, of course, related. Control of office building was, as we have noted, added in 1964. In the seventies, however, the tendency has been both to relax the limits of new floor area above which an industrial development certificate was necessary, and, to exempt all but the more prosperous regions from its operation.

This trend is the opposite of that to be seen elsewhere. The French government instituted a rather similar control of industrial building in the Paris region in 1955; it introduced control of office building in 1969; a system of graded building-permit fees and a payroll tax have also been introduced. In 1971, the Italian government imposed on industrialists in congested areas the obligation to give notice of major expansion schemes, and to submit to a 25 per cent surcharge on its construction costs if the scheme in question was deemed to violate the national plan. At least one major scheme has since been blocked as a result of this. The Netherlands government, as we have noted, proposed to operate from 1975 a licensing system on industrial and commercial building in the Randstad area, with a tax, in addition, in Rotterdam. The Swedish government introduced in 1971 a system (rather ineffective, as it proved) by which enterprises proposing to expand in Stockholm, Goteborg or Malmo were obliged to consult with the government, with a view, presumably, to allowing themselves to be diverted elsewhere. In 1974 a Royal Commission recommended comprehensive control over industrial location, on something like the (1947) British model.

The British and continental degrees of reliance upon prohibitions and disincentives have thus been, so to speak, coming to meet each other; but they have still some way to go. The British system of control, which in practice gives the opportunity for a great deal of persuasion (such as the Swedes failed to exercise for lack of sanctions, but which the Italians have used since 1968 under the title 'negotiated planning') remains the most comprehensive. The moral to be drawn from the combined experience of these countries is probably that a combination of incentives with disincentives or negative controls is necessary for implementing a regional policy in a country where the government is not in a position simply to direct industry where to go. It certainly seems likely that such a combination is stronger than the sum of its parts; firms do not adequately consider the advantages (including those provided by government incentives) that they might derive from expanding somewhere other than in their well-known neighbourhood unless they are faced with the possibility that their first choice may be blocked; prohibitions on expanding in congested regions are less likely to result in curtailment of national economic growth if the alternative is made palatable by some kind of government help.

REGIONAL POLICY VERSUS REGIONALISM

The administrative machinery by which regional policy is operated could hardly be discussed within the limits of this book. One point about it is, however, worth making, obvious though it may seem. Regional policy is necessarily a function of central governments. A good deal of confusion arises between 'regionalism', in the sense of some measure of regional self-government, and 'regional policy' in the sense in which we have been discussing it here. The two things are quite different – indeed, they may be antipathetic. What is wanted by, or what is acceptable to, the people of a region as a whole may be best discovered if there are regional institutions that are in the relevant sense representative – though for this purpose it is not necessary that they should be institutions with governmental powers. But regional policy is largely concerned with accommodating differences of interest between regions. If the provision of incentives to incoming enterprises were left to regional governments, for instance, the only possible result would be one advantageous to those with the largest per capita revenues in relation to their commitments; in fact, the most affluent. That is the kind of result that breaks up nations. Whatever powers are given to regional governments to formulate regional plans (i.e. plans for development within the region), the function of making these plans consistent with one another, and engineering the inter-regional transfers of funds and factors of production for which in their integrated totality they call, must be performed at the centre. The whole process of arriving at a regional policy is greatly helped, also, if the initiative in proposing broad (and consistent) regional planning targets comes in the first place from the centre.

Indeed, quite apart from what is generally thought of as 'regional policy', the integration of a region into the fabric of a national system of public finance tends to give it some advantages that are lost when it becomes financially independent. If a region suffers a fall in external demand for its goods, for instance, and is part of a country in which there is a centrally financed system of social insurance, the purchasing power of its population will, to a substantial extent, be maintained, partly by unemployment benefits paid into it from central funds, partly through the reduction in the taxation it is called upon to pay to the centre. More than half of the fall in its external revenue may well be cushioned in this way. The same region made financially independent, with its unemployment benefits paid for out of its own resources, might achieve the same degree of stabilisation in the face of a fall in its external revenue, but only by somehow borrowing outside to finance its consequential balance-of-payments deficit – a deficit which in an integrated national economy is financed automatically by reduced external tax payments and increased receipts of external benefits, in the way we have just described. Moreover, integration into a modern national economy produces not only a degree of stabilisation of income within the component regions, over time, but a substantial degree of inter-regional equalisation of incomes. Northern Ireland, the poorest region of the United Kingdom, has its capital formation and the disposable personal incomes of its residents supplemented by something like a fifth through the ordinary workings of national taxation and national social service expenditure, quite apart from subsidies paid under the heading of 'regional policy'. Scotland benefits to perhaps half this extent, in relation to its total income.

To these benefits of automatic stabilisation and (for the poorer regions) automatic subsidy to their standard of living there may be added other advantages brought about by national government expenditure within them, notably expenditure on such objects as defence industries and defence establishments in the region. These are not, of course, automatic benefits that come to needy regions because they are needy; they fall according to the accidents of military geography, but in particular cases they can be far more important than benefits flowing from regional policy in the ordinary sense. In the United States, for instance, total personal incomes in two states – Hawaii and Alaska – come to the extent of something like a quarter or a fifth directly from Department of Defense payrolls. Central government activities affect regional prosperity in many ways, of which regional policy accounts for only a part.

NATIONAL PROBLEMS AND NATIONAL STYLE

It is implicit in all this that the fundamental ingredients of regional policy have been mixed in very different proportions and total quantities in different countries, according to the nature of their problems and their political and social structures and traditions. The United States shows the effect of its continental scale, its federal structure, the high mobility of its people (who, as we have noted, move house almost twice as often as the British, and over greater distances in scale with the country) and its traditional *laissez-faire* doctrine that government economic intervention is a matter for crisis situations only. Regional policy, as in the United Kingdom, takes much of its character from the economic crisis of the thirties. Perhaps, in particular, the Tennessee Valley Authority set precedents in area development or redevelopment that have in some degree been followed in more recent policy; the agency operating across state boundaries with federal funds, the emphasis on co-ordinated development of natural resources and provision of infrastructure (more recently, as we have noted, public health investments, techincal education and training), the preference for acting through, or in collaboration with, local authorities, though there has been nothing lately corresponding to the TVA's massive public enterprise as a producer of electric power. There has been some aid to private enterprises by loan, but its part in American regional policy generally is not large. Financial incentives to industry to move play very little part, and negative control of industrial expansion virtually none.

Italy presents some parallels where her problem is one of area development. The operation through a special agency (the Cassa per il Mezzogiorno) with high spending power, which nevertheless worked to a large extent through subventions to local authorities (but kept large strategic schemes in its own hands), is not unlike the American approach, and with the establishment of provincial governments in Italy the resemblance has perhaps become closer. But the use of state-owned or virtually state-owned industry as the spearhead of development in the south is something that has not been possible to the same extent in any of the other countries at which we have looked (least of all in the United States), and Italy has also, as we have seen, used incentives to private industry on an increasing, and recently large, scale and, more tardily and timidly, negative controls linked with persuasion. Whatever the shortcomings of the results attained with it, this is an armoury of weapons not unworthy of a task which has, at times, been recognised as the most urgent one confronting the country.

France has also, as we have seen, used a full armoury of weapons in her regional policy: prohibitions, infrastructure and incentives, with the administrative advantage of a highly central- ised structure of government, and with the advantage, also, of a close relation between government officials and industrialists, partly rooted in the higher education system, but nurtured by the style of national economic planning developed since the war. This has enabled persuasion to do a good deal about the location of new plants and extensions that, in other countries, has been done, if at all, by more formal policy instruments. Inside the govern- ment machine, perhaps the most distinctive French device for giving regional policy a high priority has been the entrusting of the direct responsibility for it to a special unit, DATAR, within the prime minister's office, itself. All this has produced a more powerful regional policy than a mere examination of the incen- tives and prohibitions that have been in force would suggest.

Spain, like France, has a centralised government, and like both France and Italy has been undergoing very rapid urbanisa- tion. Subsidies seem to have been of some importance, but pro- hibitions less so; we noted earlier that industry seems to have been guided to some extent by where the infrastructure was, as in less developed countries, but Spain with her three or more separate coastal, industrial nuclei, and much coastal tourist development, has not been unduly worried about excessive growth of a single metropolis.

West Germany, of which we have not had occasion to say much in earlier chapters, shows a very different approach to regional

194

policy. The country's constitution makes it a federation with much power in the states: not, as we have seen, a situation that in itself makes regional policy easy. On the other hand, the constitution imposes on the Federation the task of creating and maintaining equality of living standards in all parts of the country, the tradition of governmental discrimination in its dealings with industry is deeply entrenched, and a federal structure, because it goes with regional self-consciousness, is in any case apt to create pressure for regional policy. The zone bordering on East Germany, where the new frontier disrupted old economic connections, has received very substantial aid; so have numerous development centres mostly in agricultural districts elsewhere (such as Schleswig-Holstein). German regional problems, however, have not been severe, or at least have not remained severe for long, despite the great disturbances from population movements in the fifties. The large urban concentrations centred on Hamburg, the Rhine-Ruhr, the Rhine-Main and the Rhine-Neckar confluences, and on Stuttgart, are sufficiently numerous and scattered to relieve the country of the embarrassment of having only one or two metropolitan growing points, and no area is really remote. West Germany could well qualify as a single megalopolitan area, like that stretching from Washington to Boston. Policy has been to promote a dispersed industrialisation, and expenditure on subsidies has been liberal by the standards of any other country. The approach has largely been that of the physical planner rather than the economist; to the British reader what has been written on the subject is more reminiscent of the literature on strategic plans for the English south-east than of discussions on nationwide regional policy in other countries.

This brings us to the countries of north-west Europe, of which we have given some attention in previous chapters to the United Kingdom, the Netherlands and Sweden. Their problems are different: in the United Kingdom old industrial areas handicapped largely by structural factors and a metropolitan region thought to be congested; in the Netherlands a rapid decline of agricultural employment and a central urban aggregation also, for somewhat different reasons, felt to be in need of restraint; in Sweden the problem of a small population in a large area, threatening to concentrate itself and leave great tracts almost uninhabited. But their political systems have a good deal in common: all three have used both incentives and negative controls, but the latter have been very much more important in the United Kingdom than in the other two countries, partly, perhaps, because of the traumatic shock of the interwar regional problem, from which the British policy was born, in conditions of heavy unemployment and little industrial growth, and the immediate postwar atmosphere of urgency and physical control in which it passed its most formative stage. In all three it is through the ordinary departments of the central government that policy has been carried out, rather than by special agencies, and physical infrastructure planning and growth-point philosophy have been the junior rather than the senior partners in the process.

DEGREES OF SUCCESS

Finally, what success has regional policy had in the countries from which we have drawn our examples? Like all questions of this kind, it is difficult to answer because one is comparing what actually happened with a rather shadowy hypothesis of what would have happened in the absence of the policy in question. Attempts to measure the degree of success seem to have been made systematically only for the United Kingdom and the Netherlands. In the former, two separate investigations leave little room for doubt that, between the late fifties and the late sixties, there was both a substantial change in the distribution of new industrial building in favour of the assisted areas, and, after allowing for the difference between their industrial structure and that of the rest of the country, a substantial increase in employment in them relative to the rest. There was also a statistically highly significant change in the destination to which moves of manufacturing industry (including the formation of branches) took place: the proportion going to the assisted areas rose from a quarter to over half. It can be very broadly estimated that, in the absence of any regional policy at all, the United Kingdom assisted regions would have had a growth in total employment lower by some 70,000–100,000 a year than that which they experienced in the late sixties. For Scotland, this would almost certainly have meant a net decline in population, possibly of the order of 0·5 per cent a year.

The Netherlands investigation (by Vanhove) is based upon the rate of growth of industrial employment in the various areas of the country between 1950 and 1960. For the areas in general, this growth is explained fairly well statistically by their unemployment rate (a positive influence), and their average income per head (a negative one). Most of the assisted areas, however, have done better than this general relation would suggest; Vanhove thinks that about a third of their growth may be credited to policy. A later and more restricted study by Hendriks suggests that, in the years 1960-7, about half the increase of industrial and service employment in the assisted Groningen area may have been due to the assistance it received.

Thus, in these two countries, where the change in the patterns of employment growth and (in the Netherlands) migration seems to create a *prima facie* presumption that policy has had considerable effects, this presumption is supported by studies that try to take some account of other factors at work. Elsewhere, there is little to go on except *prima facie* presumptions. One can perhaps draw some presumptions of a vague kind from the scale on which financial or fiscal inducements have been employed, where these inducements have been the chief instruments, but this does not take account of any effect of either positive controls or the distribution of infrastructure investment. For what it is worth, however, one may note that British assistance in the development areas, at either of its two peaks, in the sixties and the seventies, has amounted to capital subsidies of 15–20 per cent and labour subsidies of 5–7 per cent. French subsidies, on investment in the area of maximum benefit, lie in the range 20–30 per cent. Italian capital subsidy, counting the various benefits roughly together, runs all the way from perhaps 15 per cent on large projects to perhaps 60 per cent on small ones. Dutch capital subsidies, from the late sixties, have been initially at a rate of 25 per cent (then discretionary beyond a fairly modest maximum); Swedish subsidies, in the Inner Zone of the north, though difficult to reckon on a comparable basis, because they are partly related to employment, are probably also of the order of 20–30 per cent of capital invested, so are German subsidies in the most favoured assisted areas.

Very roughly, these subsidies amount to somewhere around a tenth of the net output of the enterprise in a typical instance (more, of course, in some capital-intensive cases), and they are of broadly the same order of magnitude between countries. One is tempted, therefore, to guess that they might have the same sort of effect as has been estimated in the British or Dutch cases; but, as we have said, this would be dangerous. Since the direct control exercised through British industrial development certificates is rather more powerful than comparable controls in the other countries, one might expect the effectiveness of their policies to be rather less than a comparison of rates of subsidy would suggest; where (in Italy and France, especially) the distribution of infrastructure investment might be expected to be rather more weighty as an influence on development than it is in the already highly urbanised, and slow-growing, United Kingdom, and if it pulls in the same direction as the inducements, the opposite might be the case. (In fact, the natural presumption that it *does* pull in the same direction, in the French case, has been challenged; Prud'homme has shown that infrastructure investment in the regions departs from its national relationship with size and growth of population in directions that bear no relation to whether the region was an assisted one or a congested one. But this may be too simple; congested regions, for instance, are well known to be greedy of such investment, and may well be given more of it than others receive without having their wants satisfied to the same extent.)

All one can really say is that, from all these indications, there seems reason to think that regional policy, as it has been pursued in the countries of Western Europe in recent years, has a very substantial effect. Where other forces have been working in the same direction (as, for instance, the forces that tend to make congestion self-limiting in the urban areas that really are congested), some quite spectacular changes have occurred: the flight of manufacturing industry out of Paris; the reversal of the previous net migration into Stockholm, the Dutch Randstad and the English south-east. On the other hand, observers have been discouraged to see that the lower income of the Italian south, the high unemployment of the north of England and western Scotland, do not vanish in a few years. We have seen why this should be so. Policy can quite quickly have an effect upon the flows of people and of jobs; it takes much longer to change the inter-regional differences of economic opportunity, rooted largely in differences of economic structure, which can be altered only slowly, or in some cases in locational advantages or disadvantages, which may yield, if at all, only to technological change.

The most important thing to understand about regional policy is that it is not for the most part a means of quickly, and once and for all, putting right a disposition of people and jobs that was wrong; it is a means of moderating the effects that arise from long-term changes taking place against various frictions, or, sometimes, of a more-or-less permanent tendency towards mislocation that has to be equally permanently resisted. It has arisen in the last two generations to an important place among the economic concerns of governments in a great many countries, largely because the economic structure of the world is changing fast. We must expect it to stay with us indefinitely.

References
and Further Reading

CHAPTER 1

The discussion in this chapter is mainly introductory. The aspect of regional economics to which it pays least attention is the theory of the location of economic activity, with which most books on the subject begin. An excellent and readable general treatment of this is to be found in E. M. Hoover, *The Location of Industrial Activity* (New York, 1948), a more formal one in H. W. Richardson, *Regional Economics* (London, 1969), Chapters 3–5, and an excellent summary by W. Alonso in Friedman and Alonso (eds), *Regional Development and Planning: a reader* (MIT Press, 1964) reprinted in Needleman (ed.), *Regional Analysis* (Penguin Modern Economics, London, 1968).

Two particular points to which reference is made rest on fuller treatment in A. J. Brown, *The Framework of Regional Economics in the United Kingdom* (Cambridge, 1972). On the relative importance of inter-regional and inter-personal inequality (p. 18 above) see Brown, pp. 81–4, and on the loss of income through mislocation of factors of production (p. 22 above) see Brown, pp. 245–9.

For a useful general introduction (with bibliography) to the more usual theoretical approaches to regional economics, see H. W. Richardson, *Elements of Regional Economics* (Penguin Modern Economics, London, 1969), though the attentive reader will notice there some important differences from the analytical background of the present book. A more 'applied' approach is E. M. Hoover, *An Introduction to Regional Economics* (New York, 1971).

CHAPTER 2

There is a considerable literature on 'shift and share' analysis (pp. 35–8 above) of inter-regional differences of economic averages. A brief account is given in Brown, op. cit., pp. 131–5. Myrdal's views on the dynamic aspects of inter-regional economic balance, referred to on p. 38 above, are in G. Myrdal, *Economic Theory and Under-developed Regions* (London, 1957).

The theory of optimal-sized aggregations of population and industry (pp. 42 above) is developed in Brown, op. cit., pp. 164–73; see also references under Chapter 7 below.

REFERENCES AND FURTHER READING

For the cyclical behaviour of systems governed by capital-stock adjustment and the multiplier, see R. C. O. Matthews, *The Trade Cycle* (Cambridge, 1958), p. 55 and Brown, op. cit., p. 200.

CHAPTER 3

For a general survey of the condition and growth of developing countries in the 1960s see United Nations, *World Economic Survey 1969-70*. On the urban problems of the 'Third World' a good brief summary is provided by Alan Mountjoy, 'March of the peasants from land to city', *Geographical Magazine*, February 1974.

A classification of problem regions somewhat similar to the present one, but confined to the United States, is that of Benjamin Chinitz, 'The Regional Problems of the United States' in E. A. G. Robinson (ed.), *Backward Areas in Advanced Countries* (London, 1969).

The greater part of the present chapter, however, is an introductory discussion of topics dealt with in later chapters, on which suggestions for further reading are to be found below.

CHAPTER 4

For the background of the East Anglian agricultural problem areas see Department of Economic Affairs, East Anglia Economic Planning Council, *East Anglia: A Study* (HMSO, 1968).

For that of central Wales see Welsh Office, *Wales: The Way Ahead* (Cmnd 3334, HMSO, 1967), and of the Scottish Highlands and Islands, Scottish Office, *The Scottish Economy 1965 to 1970* (Cmnd 2864, HMSO, 1966), and David Turnock, *Scotland's Highlands and Islands* (Problem Regions of Europe, Oxford, 1974).

An account of the problems of northern Sweden is given by Erik Bylund, 'Policy of localisation and problems of sparsely populated areas in Sweden' in E. A. G. Robinson (ed.), *Backward Areas in Advanced Countries* (London, 1969). See also W. R. Reed, *The Scandinavian Northlands* (Problem Regions of Europe, Oxford, 1974).

The problems of southern Italy have been dealt with in numerous works, of which one of the fullest is K. Allen and M. C. McLennan, *Regional Problems and Policies in Italy and France* (London, 1971), useful also for French problems of this kind; but see also, on one French problem region, Hugh Clout, *The Massif Central* (Problem Regions of Europe, Oxford, 1973), while Alan Mountjoy's work *The Mezzogiorno* in the same series summarises much of the Italian problem well. A brief account of the Spanish problem is given in H. W. Richardson, 'Regional development policy in Spain,' *Urban Studies*, 1971; but fuller accounts of European agrarian problems are to be found in the series of OECD publications appearing from 1961 onwards, notably *Low Incomes in Agriculture; Problems and Policies* (1964), *Agriculture and Economic Growth* (1965), *Agricultural Development in Southern Europe* (1969) and *Salient Features of Regional Development in Italy* (1970). See also the chapters by P. Saraceno, F. Vito and E. von Böventer in Robinson, op. cit., and U. Papi and C. Nunn (eds), *Economic Problems of Agriculture in Industrial Society* (1969).

On the south of the United States see US Department of Commerce, Economic Development Administration, *The Industrialisation of Southern Rural Areas*, 1969. On the convergence of regional incomes in the United States see Easterlin, 'Regional Growth of Income' in Kuznets, Miller and Easterlin, *Population Redistribution and Economic Growth, US, 1870–1950* (1960) and Borts and Stein, 'Regional Growth and Maturity in the United States' in Needleman (ed.), *Regional Analysis* (1969).

CHAPTER 5

A useful account of European energy policy which is an important part of the general background is R. L. Gordon, *Evolution of Energy Policy in Western Europe* (New York, 1970). Some account of problems and measures resulting from the decline of coal mining in Wales is to be found in *Wales, The Way Ahead*, already referred to. For the west Durham coalfield, a good study (though now nearly a generation old) is G. H. J. Daysh and J. S. Symonds, *West Durham: A Case Study of a Problem Area in North-East England* (Oxford, 1953), and a detailed official study of the redeployment of labour from a pit in north-east England is Department of Employment and Productivity, *Ryhope: A Pit Closes – a Study in Redeployment* (HMSO, 1970). For Belgium see L. E. Davin's chapter 'The structural crisis of a regional economy – a Case Study: the Walloon Area' in Robinson, op. cit. For the European Economic Community countries generally, there are substantial official studies in EEC, *Structures Socio-Economiques des Régions Minières et Sidérurgiques* (2 vols) (1968) and *Réadaption des Travailleurs et Réconversion des Régions* (1968).

For the United States, there are accounts of particular coal-mining areas' problems in T. R. Ford (ed.), *The Southern Appalachian Region* (Kentucky, 1962), R. C. Estall, 'West Virginia as a case study in the Appalachian regional development problem' (*Geography*, 1968), and G. E. Deasy and R. R. Greiss, 'Effects of a declining mining economy in the Pennsylvania anthracite region' (*Annals of the Association of American Geographers*, 1965).

CHAPTER 6

The discussion of 'structural' and 'regional' influences in growth (or 'shift and share analysis') calls for the same references as are mentioned in connection with the early part of Chapter 2. Reference should also be made, however, to the important United States study by H. S. Perloff, E. S. Dunn, E. E. Lampard and R. F. Muth, *Regions, Resources and Economic Growth* (Baltimore, 1960) and V. R. Fuchs, *Changes in the Location of Manufacturers in the US since 1929* (New Haven, 1962). G. H. Borts and J. L. Stein, *Economic Growth in a Free Market* (New York, 1964) discuss the point also as it relates to the United States; Brown, op. cit., discusses it for the United Kingdom. For France it is discussed in two articles by M. Beaud: 'Une analyse des disparités régionales de croissance', and 'Analyse régionale-structurale et planification régionale', both in *Revue Economique*, 1966.

On the decline of the Lancashire cotton industry see Lancashire and Merseyside Industrial Development Association, *The Decline of the Cotton and Coalmining Industries in Lancashire* (1967), and C. Miles, *Lancashire Textiles* (Cambridge, 1968). On the economy of north-east Lancashire, see Ministry of Housing and Local Government, *Central Lancashire New Town: Impact on North-East Lancashire* (HMSO, 1968), and on the upper (Yorkshire) Calder valley, Yorkshire and Humberside Economic Planning Council and Board, *Halifax and Calder Valley* (HMSO, 1968).

On the textile industries of the Nord département, the references tend to be scattered but Hugh Clout, *The France–Belgium Border Region* (Problem Regions of Europe, Oxford, 1975) gives a useful general account.

On New England, however, there are R. E. Eisenmenger, *The Dynamics of Growth in New England's Economy*, 1870–1964 (Middleton, Conn., 1967), R. C. Estall, *New England: A Study in Industrial Adjustment* (London, 1966) and G. F. Floyd (for the Office of Economic Research, Economic Development Administration), *The Changing Structure of Employment and Income in the New England Region* (1971).

More generally for the textile industries, the International Labour Organisation, Textiles Committee, 8th Session 1968, *General Report, Events and Development in the Textile Industry* may be consulted.

Much of the general background of production and trade in textiles may be gathered from Maizels, *Industrial Growth and World Trade* (Cambridge, 1963).

CHAPTER 7

The problems (largely congestion problems) of large cities are discussed by Ursula K. Hicks in *The Large City: A World Problem* (London, 1974), mostly with reference to Japan and the less developed countries, and G. Breese, *The City in Newly Developing Countries* (Englewood Cliffs, 1969) is very useful. A short discussion related particularly to London is given in Brown, op. cit., pp. 173–5 following the theoretical consideration of optimum size referred to in the notes on Chapter 2. For an introduction to the wider theory of urban economics see H. W. Richardson, *Urban Economics* (Penguin Modern Economics, London, 1971). For a variety of approaches, see two special issues of *Urban Studies*, February and October 1972. The pioneer attempt to quantify congestion costs is G. M. Neutze, *Economic Policy and the Size of Cities* (New York, 1967). The major work on urban transport problems is J. R. Meyer, J. F. Kain and M. Wohl, *The Urban Transportation Problem* (Harvard, 1965). W. J. Baumol's article 'Macroeconomics of unbalanced growth: the anatomy of urban crisis' in the *American Economic Review*, 1967, is also useful.

On the south-eastern region of England, see *Strategic Plan for the South East* (S-E Regional Planning Team, London, 1971). On the Paris region, Ian B. Thompson, *The Paris Basin* (Problem Regions of Europe, Oxford, 1973) will be found useful; see also Gravier's classic *Paris et le Désert Francais* (Paris, 1947); and on the Dutch 'Randstad', G. R. P. Lawrence's work *Randstad, Holland* (Problem Regions of Europe, Oxford, 1973) gives useful background. On the American urban problem, there is a considerable literature, some of the best contributions being in Perloff and Wingo (eds), *Issues in Urban Economics* (Baltimore, 1968), and a good summary of American discussion (with references for further reading) is the first chapter of J. L. Sundquist, *Dispersing Population* (Washington, 1975) also referred to below. The pioneer work on this, as on other aspects of regional economics is *Report of the Royal Commission on the Distribution of the Industrial Population* (the 'Barlow Report', Cmnd 6153, HMSO, 1940).

CHAPTER 8

This literature of regional policy is extensive. For the non-specialist, two books of especial value are, for general accounts and assessments, Niles Hansen (ed.), *Public Policy and Regional Economic Development: The Experience of Nine Western Countries* (Cambridge, Mass., 1974), and, on policy relating to concentration and dispersion, J. L. Sundquist, *Dispersing Population: What America Can Learn from Europe*

(Washington, 1975). For the EEC countries, important sources are, Commission of the European Communities, *Regional Development in the Community: Analytical Survey* (1971) and *Report on the Regional Problems in the Enlarged Community* (1973).

Of separate countries, the United Kingdom is covered, up to 1968, by McCrone, *Regional Policy in Britain* (London, 1969), and more briefly, up to 1971, by Brown, op. cit. (1972). For a general survey, as well as an examination of the intermediate areas, see Department of Economic Affairs, *The Intermediate Areas* (the 'Hunt Report', Cmnd 3998, HMSO, 1969). France is dealt with in Niles Hansen, *French Regional Planning* (Cambridge, Mass., 1968) and, along with Italy, in Allen and McLennan, *Regional Problems and Policies in Italy and France* referred to in the notes on Chapter 4. For the United States, see J. H. Cumberland, *Regional Development; Experiences and Prospects in the USA* (New York, 1971); G. C. Cameron, *Regional Economic Development: The Federal Role* (Resources for the Future, 1970); S. A. Levitan, *Federal Aid to Depressed Areas* (Baltimore, 1964); and D. N. Rothblatt, *Regional Planning, the Appalachian Experience* (Lexington, 1971).

On 'growth-centre' strategy, there is a United Nations series (UNRISD) including volumes by Bernard on Bulgaria and France (1970) and by H. M. Hansen on the United States (1971), and the European Free Trade Association produced a report: *Regional Policy in EFTA: An Examination of the Growth Centre Idea* (1968).

The assessments of the success of regional policy referred to in this chapter are to be found, for the UK, in Brown, op. cit., Chapter 11, and in Moore and Rhodes, 'Evaluating the effects of British regional policy' (*Economic Journal*, March 1973). For the Netherlands, the work of Vanhove and of Hendriks himself is described in Hendriks' chapter 'Regional policy in the Netherlands' in Hansen's collection *Public Policy and Regional Development* referred to above.

INDEX

Activity rates 111, 114, 136

Agglomerations, *see* Congested regions

Aggregations 39–43; benefits and disbenefits 39, 42, 158–66; and cumulative tendencies 49; and optimal size 157–61; process 40–3 (*see* congestion)

Agricultural problem regions 66–92, 119; United Kingdom 69–75; Northern Sweden 75–6; Southern Italy 77–82; West France 82–5; Rural Spain 85–7; West Germany 87–9; Southern United States 89–92; and policy 81–2, 88; *see also* rural regions, population, migration, unemployment *and* employment

Agriculture 34, 44, 66–9; colonisation 75; employment Chapter 4 *passim*; and pressure on land 33, 54, 63, 66, 79; and productivity 66–9, 80, 88, 90; and subsistence sector 52–6, 66

American cities 163–4, 168; and policy 171, 178

Appalachia 108–9, 112, 115, 180, 187

Barlow Commission 28, 162, 173

Basic and nonbasic employment 34–5, 139

Beckerman, W. 44

Belgium 61, 64, 97, 99, 111, 114, 116, 128

Borts, G. H. and Stein, J. L. 91, 124

Building controls 84, 167, 173–7, 190–1, 197–8

Capital: accumulation 30–4, 43–7, 64; distribution 21, 30; labour ratio 22; mobility 18–19, 32–3, 37–8 (*see* industrial movement); output ratios 44–6; productivity 18, 32–3; Stock adjustment 43–7

Cassa per il Mezzogiorno 184, 193–4

Classification, problem regions 51–65

Coal industry 58, 93–7; and early retirement 111, 112; and government policies 116–18; and physical location 58, Chapter 5 *passim*

Coalmining regions 37, 93–118, 119; activity rates 114; adjustments 105–9; Belgium 97, 99, 101, 107, 111, 114, 116; and derelict land 115; and female employment 112–15; France 97, 101, 103, 107, 111, 113–15; output and growth 97–9; Regional dependence 99–105, 108; and regional policy 110, 116–18; Ruhr 103, 107–8, 112; and unemployment 110–12; United Kingdom 101–3, 106–7, 109, 110, 113; United States 105, 108–9, 112, 114 (*see also* employment, migration, population, incomes)

Complementary region 15

Congested regions: in developing countries 61, 62; in developed countries 62–5, 151–69; *see also* aggregation, urban areas, regional policy, employment, population, unemployment

Congestion: and advantages of scale 156–7, 166; brake on congestion 155, 166–9; concern at concentration 161–6; definitions 151–2; and optimal regional population 160–1, 166; and optimal urban size 157–60, 166, 168–9, 170; traffic 155–6; and urban size 41–3, 152–6; and urban costs 162–3, 164, 165

Cumulative causation models 38–50; dynamic mechanisms 43–7; economies of scale 38–43; and policy 48–50; public finance mechanism 48

Printed in the United States
by Baker & Taylor Publisher Services